CISTERCIAN AND MENDICANT MONASTERIES IN MEDIEVAL GREECE

CISTERCIAN ❦ ❦ ❦
AND MENDICANT ❦
MONASTERIES IN ❦
MEDIEVAL GREECE

Beata Kitsiki Panagopoulos

THE UNIVERSITY OF CHICAGO PRESS · *Chicago & London*

BEATA KITSIKI PANAGOPOULOS is associate professor of art and architectural history at San José State University and has written several articles in her field.

The University of Chicago Press, Chicago 60637
The University of Chicago Press, Ltd., London
© 1979 by The University of Chicago
All rights reserved. Published 1979
Printed in the United States of America
83 82 81 80 79 5 4 3 2 1

Library of Congress Cataloging in Publication Data
Panagopoulos, Beata Maria, 1925–
    Cistercian and mendicant monasteries in medieval Greece.
    Bibliography: p.
    Includes index.
    1. Monasteries—Greece, Medieval. 2. Architecture, Cistercian—Greece, Medieval. 3. Architecture, Gothic—Greece, Medieval. 4. Church architecture—Greece, Medieval. I. Title.
NA5593.P36   726′.7′09495   78–10769
ISBN 0–226–64544–4

To my parents, Nikos and Beata Kitsiki

Contents

Illustrations

Maps

Plates

Illustrations

Preface

This work is a general study of the most important Gothic monasteries and churches built in Greece by the Franks and the Venetians during the thirteenth, fourteenth, and fifteenth centuries. Though we have a few monographs on several monuments and regions of Greece, so far no general work has examined and compared them architecturally, stylistically, and historically. The only important study is A. Bon's *La Morée Franque,* which discusses in great detail the religious architecture of the Peloponnesus.[1] Nothing similar exists for the rest of Greece except for Crete, whose monuments were extensively cataloged at the beginning of this century by G. Gerola.[2] The monuments of Cyprus have been thoroughly studied by C. Enlart and again by R. B. Francis.[3]

This book will focus on the unity of religious architecture during those centuries when builders had many common characteristics and will examine Greece's monuments in detail.

As in other European countries, from Scandinavia to Spain and Italy and from England to Hungary, the monastic orders in Greece used Gothic forms in their buildings beginning at the end of the twelfth century. In countries other than Greece, a new synthesis slowly evolved during the thirteenth century, producing a Gothic art with a different personality in each country. In Greece, however, both on the continent and in Cyprus, the monastic orders introduced French Gothic techniques. On the other islands this task was the work of the mendicant orders, with Venice as intermediary.

The constructions of the Franks[4] and the Venetians in Greece show a family resemblance, as do the abbeys of the Cistercians and the mendicant orders across Europe. Their aesthetics, following the rules and principles of their orders, express humility and simplicity and easily adapt themselves to the artistic concepts common to Mediterranean regions.

Thus, parallel to the Gothic Rayonnant style of the thirteenth and fourteenth centuries, where the sense of matter and volume disappears, one sees mural values reappearing in the monastic churches: the organization of lines and forms is subject to logic, height is subordinate to width, and almost all have a two-story elevation with pointed arches and ribbed vaults.

At a time when one finds lacy surfaces in other Gothic constructions, primarily in the north of Europe, the aesthetics of these Mediterranean buildings retain a monumental simplicity that reminds one of the early Christian basilicas. Across Europe and down to Greece the monastic orders strung a rosary of houses of prayer whose architecture is stripped of unnecessary detail. By contrast with the notion of the cosmos or the "divine Jerusalem" expressed in the northern Gothic churches, these monastic churches manifest an almost antimedieval spirit. Yet one can hardly doubt that this architecture constitutes a true aspect of the Gothic, rather than a bastardized expression of Romanesque art or an impoverished version of the richer Gothic style. But it is a very different aesthetic expression, adapted not only to each diverse region but also to the particular needs of the monks.

In Greece this Western architecture spread with the Catholic faith as a result of the great papal dream of a religious union of East and West under Rome. Innocent III, who had encouraged the Fourth Crusade to save the Holy Land from the infidels, resigned himself to the conquest of Constantinople as the Crusade deviated from its goal. Alexis Comnenos, son of the deposed emperor of Constantinople, had promised the Crusaders at the siege of Zara (1202) that, if they helped him dethrone the usurper, he would help impose the authority of the pope in the Byzantine Empire. He did not keep his promise, though Innocent III tried on several occasions to persuade Alexis III to bring the Greek church under obedience to Rome. When in 1204 a Latin emporer was elected, the pope hurried to latinize the patriarchate of Constantinople and of the Greek bishoprics.

Although he encountered serious difficulties, Innocent desired even more ardently to persuade the native population as well as the Byzantine clergy to adopt the Catholic faith and come to an agreement with the foreign clergy. For the moral and religious conquest of the Byzantine world, the papacy encouraged the Cistercian monks, hoping that their austere principles would win the respect and admiration of the native population. But by the end of the thirteenth century the Cistercians had encountered difficulties and had lost all influence, and they returned to the West. On their departure the delicate role of capturing the hearts of the Greeks was left to the mendicant orders. The Franciscans and the Dominicans, who established themselves primarily in the Greek islands, often adopted the architecture of the Cistercians but established large communities where they could preach to and mingle with a large segment of the population.

This study will primarily examine the extant religious structures, often in ruins, that were born from this expansion of monastic orders. Secondarily it will note the influence their architecture might have had on Byzantine styles. Yet if we finally conclude that Western medieval architecture was never assimilated in Greece and never created a new art influenced by this contact, there still remains the problem of why its expansion did not have the same results as in other regions where it was transplanted. As in antiquity, during this period Greek art confronted Western art and the art of the Orient. For Gothic art it constituted a remarkable expansion, with its forms spread over all of Europe and across the Mediterranean up to the Holy Land.

Acknowledgments

In 1949, when I had just come from Greece to study at the University of Chicago, I had the great good fortune to study under Professor U. A. Middeldorf, then chairman of the Art Department. It is to him that I owe my first interest in this study. At the time, my travel to study these monuments was hindered by many obstacles, but I never forgot his enthusiasm in talking to me about the Frankish castles he remembered seeing in Greece. After fifteen years and many trips to Greece, I finally started working on this study, though my interest had settled on ecclesiastical rather than military architecture. I repeatedly visited the sites, in some cases in remote areas of Greece and Cyprus, where the Latin monks had established their monasteries. I acquainted myself with the countryside, talked to local inhabitants, and took measurements and photographs of the often very damaged constructions, which in some cases were hard even to see because they were so overgrown by vegetation.

I am very thankful to the American Philosophical Society, which in 1972 gave me a grant to pursue this work in Cyprus. I also had the good fortune to have had the guidance of Professor Antoine Bon, author of *La Morée Franque,* and of Professor Jean Lassus of the Collège de France at the University of Paris.

For the Greek Service of Antiquities, unfortunately, the Frankish and Venetian periods have not played an important role, and no foreign schools of art and archaeology have been interested in excavating or restoring the monuments of this period in Greece. But, I am grateful for the support and encouragment I received personally from Professor A. Orlandos, long-time director of the Greek Service of Antiquities. I also want to thank M. E. Stikas, director of the Service of Restoration, who provided me with unpublished material on the church of Zaraka.

In some cases my work was made extremely difficult because, as a woman, I faced barriers created by religious beliefs and traditions; for instance, it was impossible for me to visit the choir and chapels behind the iconostasis in the active church of Saint Paraskevi in Chalkis. Fortunately my husband was able to take the photographs for me and also to make necessary measurements.

In Chania on the Island of Crete, I am extremely grateful to the Service of Restoration and to the director of the Service of Greek Antiquities, which were most helpful to me, and to K. E. Lassithiotakis, in Herakleion, who willingly gave his valuable time to discuss his restoration of the church of Saint Francis in Canea, which is now the Museum of Antiquities.

Professor M. Manousakas, director of the Greek Institute of Byzantine Studies in Venice, gave me the opportunity to work with documents in the possession of the institute. He pointed out special problems concerning Crete and guided me to other sources. I am also thankful for the help I received from the Kunsthistorisches Institut in Florence and from the Bibliothèque Nationale in Paris.

The quality of this publication would have suffered greatly without the photographic expertise of Makis Skiadaresis, who went with me on several trips to photograph these monasteries. He was willing to climb on roofs, hike up mountains, and drive over dusty dirt roads.

I also want to thank Dr. Margaret Burke, who helped me with some of the drawings, as well as the architect Thanos Kontopoulos. I am most grateful to Veronica Ions for her editing of the manuscript and to Professor Marion Richards for her constant advice. I also want to thank Professor Walter Horn very warmly for giving his time so unselfishly.

Most of all, though, I owe the completion of this book to my husband, E. P. Panagopoulos, who at all times supported me and who spent an incredible number of hours not only out in the field, but at home helping me with every aspect of this work.

Part One   HISTORICAL BACKGROUND

I *Political and Religious Conditions*

The Frankish Middle Ages in Greece begin with the Latin domination of Constantinople on 13 April 1204, the result of the Fourth Crusade that Pope Innocent III had urged in 1198. Venice undertook to conduct the fleet to Jerusalem, but the doge of Venice, Enrico Dandolo, diverted the course of the Crusade from Jerusalem to Constantinople. There were two reasons. Venice had long been aware of the commercial value of the Levant, having dealt with the Byzantines since the eleventh century,[1] and Dandolo had also been relying on the promises for concessions of Alexis, son of the former Byzantine emperor Isaac II, who had been dethroned by his brother. The fleet, turning around, anchored in the harbor of Constantinople, capital of the rich Byzantine Empire, and the Crusaders disembarked there instead of continuing to the Holy Land.[2] No one could have foreseen how this change of plans would change the goal of the Crusade.

The Conquest of Constantinople

Since the history of the conquest is well known from accounts by numerous chroniclers and historians,[3] I will mention only pertinent details. After reinstating the old emperor Isaac II on his throne, at the instigation of Alexis IV and his father the Franks prolonged their stay in Constantinople until the spring of 1204.[4] The inhabitants of the capital interpreted this as foreign occupation and repeatedly expressed their opposition, dangerously weakening Isaac's position on the throne.

At the beginning of Isaac's new reign, the Crusaders were convinced they had used good judgment in assisting Alexis and Isaac, for both immediately started to help the Crusaders accomplish their task in the Orient. Their ultimate goal was the conquest of Jerusalem.[5] But, with the unrest of the local population and the emperor's insecurity, the Crusaders had serious doubts that the Byzantines would ultimately help them reach the Holy Land. The Crusaders abandoned all desire to go to Palestine, and on 12 April 1204 Constantinople fell for the second time. With no great difficulty the Crusaders became its masters.

Most Greeks left the Byzantine capital for Nicea or Trebizond on the Black Sea, which became the capitals of the new empires, lasting for more than two and a half centuries.[6]

As masters of Constantinople, the Franks were obliged to choose an emperor from among themselves. They placed Baudouin, a Flemish count, at the head of the empire and gave him as his own domain a fourth of the Byzantine territory.

This division of the land was prepared by twenty-four surveyors, twelve Venetians and twelve Crusaders, among whom was Geoffrey of Villehardouin. The rest of the Byzantine Empire was divided equally between the Crusaders and the Venetians. Boniface de Monferrat, Baudouin's rival for election as emperor, received the territory east of Constantinople and the island of Crete. Boniface, however, preferred an area closer to his native land and exchanged this territory for the kingdom of Salonika and sovereignty over the major part of Greece.[7] He probably needed money to subjugate the Greek regions, and because Crete seemed too distant from the rest of his domain, since he had no fleet of his own, he tried to sell the kingdom of Crete to the Genoese.[8] Venice, however, knowing the importance of this island's maritime commerce, intervened and bought the island from Boniface for 3,000 ducats.[9]

The major part of central Greece, included among the territories ceded to the Crusaders, lay in the sphere of influence of the kingdom of Salonika and awaited conquest by Boniface and his companions. As early as the end of the year 1204, the marquis of Montferrat and several knights of different nationalities, such as Guillaume of Champlitte from Champagne, Othon de la Roche from Burgundy, Jacques of Avesnes and Jacques and Nicolas of Saint Omer from Flanders, Berthold Katzenellenbogen from the Rhine region, Guido Pallavicini from Parma, Thomas Autremencourt from the Laonnais region, and Ravano dalle Carceri from Verona[10] completed the conquest of this territory. Boniface distributed the most important provinces to the knights who had helped him during this campaign. In return, his knights owed him the same fealty they were accustomed to render in the feudal system of Western Europe.

The Franks had met very little resistance during their conquest. The Byzantine provinces were ready to accept any master, having long since been abandoned by the Byzantines. Left to their fate, they were exploited by local tyrants like the infamous Leon Sgouros, hereditary ruler of Nafplion. The historical development of each region by the Crusaders is examined later in this chapter. Here it is enough to enumerate the different fiefs distributed in Greece:

1. Principalities: The principality of Morea or Achaia, 1205–1430.

2. Duchies: The duchy of Athens, 1205–1460 and the duchy of the Archipelagos, 1207–1566.

3. Marquisate: The marquisate of Boudonitsa, 1205.

4. Counties: The county of Salona at the foot of Mount Parnassus, 1205, and the palatine county of Cephalonia, which had been in the hands of the Italians since 1194 and remained in Venetian hands until 1483.

5. The fief of Gravia in Boeotia, 1205.[11]

The lords of Burgundy, Champagne, Lombardy, and Flanders became the new princes, dukes, marquises, and counts. The merchants of Venice, who during the partition had received a considerable amount of land, formed the dominant class of the merchant colonies, established in Crete from 1205 to 1669, in Euboea at Negreponte from 1209 to 1470, and in the Cyclades from 1206 to 1540. They also succeeded in controlling certain parts of Morea, Modon, Coron, and Monemvasia, and they established themselves in the Ionian islands on the coast of Epirus and Albania, on the islands of Aegina, and at Salamis in the Gulf of Saronikos[12] (map 1).

As masters of most of the islands, of the Adriatic ports, of the Aegean Sea, and even of the Black Sea, the Venetians controlled the commercial life of the Levant. They had, however, certain rivals like the Genoese, who had also established themselves in the colonies of the Black Sea on the islands of Chios, Samos, Ikaria, and Lesbos, mostly during the end of the thirteenth century and the first half of the fourteenth century.

The Monastic Orders: Cistercians, Franciscans, Dominicans, and Military Orders in Greece

The ecclesiastical orders of the West that settled in Greece after the Fourth Crusade played as important a role as the feudal aristocracy and the Venetian and Genoese traders.

Pope Innocent III, a passionate and ardent advocate of the Fourth Crusade, encouraged the Cistercians, among others, to take an active part in it.[13] In July 1198 Innocent III instructed the abbot Luke of Lambucina to preach the Crusade in Sicily.[14] He also appears to have encouraged the Crusade in a letter to Foulques de Neuilly when the latter visited the general chapter in 1201 to ask the help of certain abbots designated by the pope.[15] Several members of the order took part in the Crusade, among them the abbot of Vaux and the abbot Peter of Lucedio.[16] In 1201, after many objections, the Cistercians promised to work for this enterprise.[17]

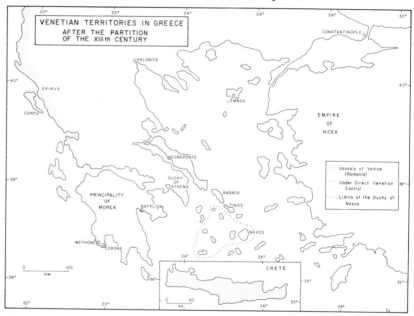

Map 1

Quite naturally, when the moment came for the partition of the empire after the conquest of Constantinople, the Cistercians were eager to take an active part. In the twelfth century they had already settled in Cyprus and in Syria.[18] Between 1204 and 1276 the order received at least twelve establishments in Constantinople and in Greece.[19] Though their monasteries did not have the long history of those in the West, they exercised at least a political influence and even played an important role as liaison between the pope and the Latin empire.

At the request of the Latin emperor of Constantinople, the Cistercian abbot Peter of Lucedio supported Boniface of Montferrat against Baudouin.[20] In return, Boniface gave the Cistercians the Greek monastery of Chortaitou, situated on the mountain near Salonika, as an offshoot of the mother house of Lucedio in Piedmont. Peter of Lucedio installed Geoffrey, one of his Cistercian brothers, as abbot, and he himself, perhaps encouraged by Boniface, became archbishop of Salonika.[21]

Other Cistercians besides Peter of Lucedio became eminent figures in the religious and political life of the Latin empire. In the first twenty years after the conquest, six Cistercian convents and two first-daughter houses of these convents were founded, then four new foundations were added. These twelve monasteries were scattered from Chalcedon to the Peloponnesus and from Euboea to Crete, but the greatest number were concentrated in Constantinople and in Morea.

During the thirteenth century, however, the Cistercian influence declined. The monastery of Chortaitou, for instance, must have lasted approximately as long as the kingdom of Salonika. We know it still existed in 1224, because in 1223 the bishop of Negreponte, with the agreement of his chapter, gave Chortaitou the Greek monastery of Euboea, Saint Archangelus of the diocese of Negreponte. In this fashion, the monastery of Chortaitou even obtained a first-daughter house.[22] In turn, Othon de la Roche of Athens (1205–25) gave the old monastery of Daphni to the Cistercians of the abbey of Bellevaux in 1207.[23] The de la Roche family had always had close relations with the Cistercian abbot of Bellevaux of the diocese of Besançon.[24] The monastery of Daphni continued to exist until 1458 (map 2).

In Crete, during 1218 the Greek monastery of Gergeri was affiliated with Saint Thomas of Torcello near Venice[25] (a Burgundian daughter house), and in 1230 a second abbey, Saint Mary Varangorum, was given to Saint Thomas by Giacomo Tiepolo, doge of Venice.[26] These monasteries were still in existence in 1273, for at that time the abbot of Saint Thomas asked the general chapter for permission to send certain brothers there.[27] Unfortunately, today there are no traces of Saint Mary Varangorum or of Saint Stephen, which was situated in the vicinity of Constantinople and also affiliated with Saint Thomas of Torcello,[28] or of the three other Cistercian monasteries known to Constantinople.[29]

It is probable that in Morea a Cistercian foundation was established before 1212 by the monks of Hautecombe of the diocese of Geneva, but one cannot be positive about its site.[30] When in 1225 Geoffrey I of Villehardouin asked the general chapter of the Cistercians to send a group of brothers to build a monastery in Achaia,[31] they chose the abbot of Morimond to lead this mission. But neither the name nor the place where the monastery was to be built are mentioned.

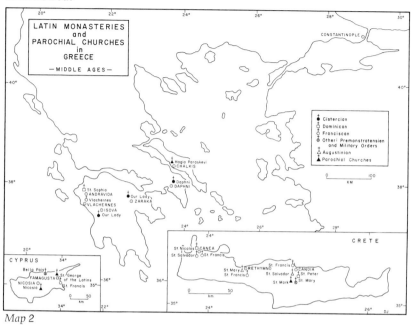

Map 2

Today the only Cistercian monastery that is positively known exists in ruins at Zaraka in Morea by Lake Stymphalia. Before 1236 it must have belonged to the diocese of Corinth.[32]

After 1276, almost all Cistercian monasteries were abandoned. At the beginning of the fourteenth century the monastery of Daphni was the only one that still existed on the mainland of Greece. In Crete, Gergeri and Saint Mary Varangorum were also active until the fourteenth century. In contrast with the Cistercian decline, the activity of the Franciscan and Dominican orders increased during the thirteenth century. Even before the restoration of the Byzantine Empire, as soon as the popes felt the strength of the Latin princes weakening, they turned toward the emperor and the patriarch of Nicea, attempting to realize the sought-for-union. The Franciscan monks, established on Greek soil, took the initiative and became the principal negotiators. During 1232, five Franciscan monks fervently negotiated a union.[33]

The Franciscans had established themselves in the Latin Empire in 1219. About the year 1220 they had a convent in Constantinople, though its exact location is not known, for it disappeared with the fall of the Latin Empire. In Greece the Franciscans were established by Benedetto of Arezzo, and soon after they created the province of "Romania," as they named it.[34] The life of the Franciscan monasteries was much longer than that of the Cistercian abbeys, which had survived only under the authority of the Latin princes and whose influence declined when the Greeks returned to Constantinople.[35]

The Dominicans or preaching friars also occupy an important place in the history of the Latin church of the Near East. The province of Greece was one of the new areas where success was eagerly anticipated both by the Dominican order and by the papacy. It was also expected to contribute to the realization of the great dream of ecclesiastical union.[36] Unfortunately, the sources on this are desperately poor. In certain regions of the "Dominican province" of Greece, as well as of Cyprus, Crete, and Rhodes, social and religious conditions continued with no great change from their establishment until the sixteenth century. From this later period we have some information that sheds light on the past.

It appears certain that the "Dominican province" in Greece completely neglected its own history. Even Venice, to which almost all the documents related to the "Venetian Romania" were transported, does not seem to have incorporated any Dominican archives from Greece. Flaminio Cornaro (Flaminius Cornelius), in his *Creta Sacra,* does not mention that even one manuscript came from the Dominicans in Crete. He drew the scanty information in his book from a Franciscan source.[37]

The Dominicans had had a convent in Constantinople until 1261, but it was destroyed when the town was reconquered by the Byzantines. They returned to the Bosporus at the end of the thirteenth century, but, the new foundation of the order at the monastery of Pera was no longer part of the province of Greece.

A document in the archives of the order lists the monasteries and their daughter houses and the number of monks during the years 1650–55. In Crete it cites four convents in the town of Candia, capital of the island. Saint Peter of Candia must have been one of the most ancient monasteries of the province and was surely founded before 1277.[38] The three others were Saint Paul, founded by Luca Ugolini,[39] Saint Mary Borozani, and Saint Catherine. Of the town of Pediada in the neighborhood of Candia, Gerola mentions the monastery of Saint George, a daughter house of Saint Peter of Candia.

At Canea are mentioned the monasteries of Saint Nicolas and the Virgin of the Miracles,[40] at Rethymno, the convent of Saint Mary Magdalene.[41] The same document notes that the Dominican province of Greece also extended over all of Morea and over several islands of the Aegean, Chios among them. In the Ionian islands he mentions the small monastery of Saint Elias on the island of Zante and Saint Rosario in Cephalonia.

The Dominican province of Greece seems never to have attracted any great number of monks. Many moral, political, and economic difficulties impeded the growth of the Dominicans. One can even say that on several occasions the religious question created such problems that it became a hindrance to the solution of many social and political issues in Greece. Naturally the situation was not always the same in the different regions of Greece, and it changed considerably under the different Latin lords—de la Roche and Ville-hardouin, as well as the Anjou and Venetians. One can, however, take the liberty of generalizing and state that the Greek population and the Greek Orthodox clergy were almost always hostile to the Latin church. The Greeks remained faithful to their own church and their own rites, and they watched the Latin church and its representatives with extreme suspicion. This was even truer in the areas governed by the Venetians, and especially in Crete, where the Latin clergy and the Venetian community were forced to remain segregated from the Greek population. For Venice, which wanted to strengthen the ties between the Catholic clergy and its political interests, it was indispensable to maintain the faith of Venetian emissaries abroad and to reduce the influence of the local priests upon them. A gulf was thus created between the Greeks and the Latins.

Simultaneously, the Latin clergy, especially the Dominican monks, lost their status because of the attitude of Venice. Instead of being zealous and obedient follower of Rome, the *Serenissima* primarily considered its own political interests and motives and more than once created obstacles that slowed down the Dominican administrative machinery. The Venetian government preferred a less enthusiastic clergy, more compliant with its own aims.

In the sixteenth century the Dominicans had about thirty monks. In the thirteenth, fourteenth, and fifteenth centuries the monasteries must have had few more, since in the documents complaints on the lack of personnel never cease.

Not only the mendicant orders and the Cistercians, but the religious military orders as well received lands and buildings all through the Latin Empire. From the very beginning of the Latin Empire the emperor, the marquis of Montferrat, and the barons generously endowed the Templars and Hospitalers. But the belligerent and eager spirit of the military orders repeatedly created difficulties.[42] The Hospitalers established themselves in 1310 on the island of Rhodes, where important vestiges of their presence remain.

The Organization of the Catholic Church in the Latin Empire: Ecclesiastical Geography

Pope Innocent III, the Venetians, and the Crusaders—the protagonists of the Fourth Crusade—agreed that establishing the Latin church in the new Frankish empire was one of the most important objectives of the conquest. But everyone looked out for his own interests first, particularly Innocent III, who was hoping to unite the church under the leadership of Rome. The pope tried to reorganize the spiritual hierarchy in the new empire diplomatically, without totally expelling the Greek clergy. The Latin church thus restricted itself to the highest posts, installing Westerners with close ties to Rome, and contented itself with token obedience from the rest of the Greek clergy. Most of the Byzantine bishops had already abandoned their thrones at the time of the invasion. The rest were displaced by the Franks.

Although the Holy See replaced the Byzantine bishops with extreme caution, the reaction of the Greek population was bitter and continuous, and the Latin church managed to establish itself in the new territories only with great disorder.

The Latin patriarchate of Constantinople was placed under the protection of Saint Peter of Rome by confirmation of the pope. The patriarch received privileges that raised him to the second position in Christendom. He was the representative of the pope in the Near East and more highly placed than the patriarchs of Alexandria, Antioch, and Jerusalem. Nevertheless, an apostolic "legate" was placed next to the patriarch, representing the pope and charged with handling every order of the patriarch.[43] This legate, in effect, held the real power. The Venetians also tried to control the new Latin church to their advantage. The first Latin patriarch, Tommaso Morosini, was a Venetian. After leaving Rome for Constantinople, Morosini stopped in Venice. Here his voyage was delayed until he promised in writing (1) to take as canon of Saint Sophia only a Venetian or a cleric who had resided in Venice at least ten years; (2) to ask his canon to promise under oath that he would elect only a Venetian patriarch; (3) to accept for the bishoprics under his jurisdiction only candidates of Venetian origin.

Although Morosini himself remained faithful to the pope, most Latin clerics were Venetians attached to Venice. This became even more apparent when the patriarch of Constantinople had to seek refuge in Negreponte after the Byzantines returned to power in the capital of the Latin Empire. Many indications reveal to what extent the Latin patriarchate of Constantinople in Negreponte remained in the hands of Venetian prelates. Similarly, the bishoprics of Venetian Greece were almost always assigned to Venetians.

The other lords who had settled in Greece were also reluctant to accept the authority of Rome. They tried in every case to avoid the obligations imposed on them by the hierarchy of the feudal society. They often took over the lands assigned to the church to build their own castles.[44] They even demanded that the church submit to the legislation they established for their own society and their fiefs—to the jurisdiction of Romania.

Confusion and disorganization were typical not only during the first years of the establishment of the Latin Empire, but also during the period that followed. The documents of this period include innumerable complaints of various kinds.[45] In describing the ecclesiastical geography of the Latin Empire, then, one must certainly remember that the patriarch of Constantinople, although officially the head of the Latin church in Greece, was in reality not always as powerful as the archbishops of Patras and of Candia or the bishop of Zante, who most often refused obedience to his superior, the archbishop of Corinth.

THE DIOCESES

The dioceses organized by the new church at first differed only slightly from those of the Byzantine church, and changes took place gradually. The bishops who had been placed in office after the establishment of the Latin church thus had to content themselves with the territory their predecessors, the Greek bishops, had held.

In several regions certain bishoprics later had to be reduced as the resources of the church became fewer and made the upkeep of a large Latin clergy impossible[46] (map 3). Northern Greece included two Latin archbishoprics, one in Salonika and the other in Philippi, whose existence was very short-lived. In central Greece there were four—at Larissa in Thessaly, Thermopylae in Phocis, Neopatra in Phtiotis, and Thebes in Boeotia. In Attica the archbishopric of Athens was as important as it had been during the

Byzantine period; among others, the Latin bishopric of Andros, one of the Aegean islands, depended on it. A Latin bishop had settled there in 1225.[47] The sources are not always precise, and not all the bishoprics of central Greece are certainly known, but there must also have been one in Davalia[48] (Davlia Daulis in antiquity) and another in Cheronea. On the island of Euboea, after the Byzantine reconquest in 1260 the bishopric of Negreponte became the seat of the Latin patriarchate displaced from Constantinople.[49]

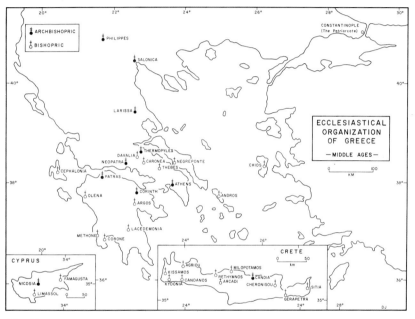

Map 3

Morea included two archbishoprics, one in Patras, which was of great political importance to the Achaian principality, and one in Corinth, established a little later, after the conquest of the Peloponnesus in 1212, and on which the bishoprics of Argos and Lacedemonia depended. The bishop of Olena, who resided in the capital of the principality, Andravida, reported to the archbishop of Patras. The name Olena was retained from the Byzantine bishopric which until the Latin conquest had its seat in the town of Olena.

Corone and Methone, as well as the Ionian islands of Zante and Cephalonia, also depended on Patras.[50] Crete, the only direct possession of Venice except for the towns of Corone and Methone in Morea, depended on Venice even in the ecclesiastical domain. The part the church received, after the political division of the island into sestieri in 1208 by Giacomo Tiepolo,[51] is difficult to evaluate, for it was not one territory but many different possessions, which were part of the property of the state and of the land given to the Venetian feudal lords.

The Latin archdiocese of Crete was established in 1212 in Candia not in the ancient Greek metropolis of Gortyna.[52] According to Flaminio Cornaro, in the thirteenth century it was divided into four bishoprics: Melopotamos (1212), Sitia (1219 or 1225), Jerapetra (1223 or 1240), and Rethymno or Calamon (1287). The bishopric of Cheronissou (Cironensis) was created in 1306, of Agriou in 1307, of Agias (Agiensis) in 1310, of Arcadi in 1330, of Chissamou in 1346, and probably of Kandanou (Canticensis)[53] also in 1346. But a reduction later occurred in the number of bishoprics in existence. In 1467–80 Kandanou was eliminated and in 1583 Agriou and Sitia.

During the thirteenth century, after the partition of the Latin Empire and the organization of the Latin church, many islands assigned to the Venetians remained in the hands of the Greeks. The islands of Chios and Lesbos, Icaria, Samos, and Psara near the coast of Asia Minor became part of the Byzantine Empire of Nicea.[54] It was only after the fourteenth century, when the Greeks returned to Constantinople, that these islands were governed by Genoese families and a Latin clergy established itself there. From that period on, Chios became the seat of a bishopric. Similarly, the island of Rhodes was conquered as late as 1309 by the Hospitalers of Saint John, who governed it along with the small neighboring islands.[55]

The island of Corfu in the Ionian Sea remained until 1267 under the rule of the Greek despot of Epirus, since the Latin church established itself there only at the end of the thirteenth century. Cyprus, on the contrary, had a Latin archbishopric in the capital of the island, Nicosia, from the end of the twelfth century, with jurisdiction over the three bishops of Paphos, Limassol, and Famagusta.

The relations of these dioceses with Saint Peter's of Rome differed considerably according to the political vicissitudes of the temporal princes.

2 *The Historical Development of the Regions Occupied by the Franks*

The study of the historical development of the Frankish period in Greece presents great difficulties. Most of the new states created by the Crusaders changed masters periodically throughout the Middle Ages.

The thirteenth century, often known as the invasion period, was mostly dominated by the Franks, whereas the fourteenth and fifteenth centuries were primarily Italian periods, when bankers and merchants replaced the knights. It was also in the fourteenth century that bands of Catalan warriors and the mercenary company of Navarre appeared in Greece.

The succession of political masters and religious orders at different periods influenced ecclesiastical building in many ways. The most interesting regions in this respect are those of central and northern Greece and of the islands.

Central Greece

The Latin Empire of Constantinople and the kingdom of Salonica, because of their short life, left no important vestiges. And the western coast of Greece from Durazzo to the Gulf of Patras, assigned to Venice during the partition of Constantinople, but never conquered, remained in the hands of the Greeks. This territory was subject to the despotism of Epirus under the lordship of a cousin of Alexis III, Michael Comnenos Dukas, and continued the Byzantine traditions. Within it there is no important Frankish monument, though one can observe a certain Italian influence on architecture and sculpture. It therefore seems meaningful to concentrate specific attention on the historical development of the regions south of Macedonia and west of the Pindus, Thessaly, Attica, the Megaris, Morea, and the islands.

In autumn 1204[1] the Venetians and the Crusaders, who had received three-quarters of the Byzantine territory (the other quarter had been assigned to the emperor Baudouin),[2] began further conquests to occupy the assigned territories. In this manner Guglielmo, a Lombard nobleman, became lord of Larissa, Guido Pallavicini became lord of Thermopylae and of Boudonitsa, Jacques and Nicolas of Staint Omer received fiefs near the pass of Gravia, and Thomas of Autremencourt received the county of Salona. Athens, Thebes, all of Attica, and Megaride were given by Boniface to his friend Othon de la Roche, a nobleman from Burgundy.

The Duchy of Athens

The duchy of Athens remained in the hands of the French until the beginning of the fourteenth century. The last duke of Athens was Gautier de Brienne, also duke of Burgundy (1308–11), who died during the battle of Orchomenos against the Catalans. As a result the duchy of Athens fell to Catalan bands who had received help from King Frederick II of Aragon. For a short time thereafter, the duchy was governed by a Sicilian duke. During the last century preceding the Turkish occupation, Athens was governed by the Florentine family of the Acciajuoli, with a short interval during the years 1395–1404, when Venice was ruling Athens.

The Principality of Morea

The Peloponnesus was conquered by two knights, William of Champlitte and Geoffrey of Villehardouin, nephew of the marshal of Champagne and of Romania.[3] The latter was sailing toward Palestine with several other knights during 1204, when a storm forced him ashore at Methone, a town of the southern Peloponnesus. He immediately came into contact with Champlitte, who was in the Peloponnesus, and by 1205 they had become the masters of Morea and had established the principality of Achaia.[4]

Champlitte became the first prince but died suddenly in 1209. Villehardouin and his descendants, Geoffrey II (1228–46) and William (1246–78), succeeded him as lords of the principality of Morea.[5] This became the most brilliant Frankish period of Achaia. Unfortunately, however, after a defeat of William of Villehardouin in 1259, part of the southeastern area of Peloponnesus had to be abandoned and the king of Sicily, Charles I of Anjou, had to be asked for help. Even worse, William died with no descendants.[6]

Thus began the second Frankish period (1278–1364), during which Morea was governed primarily by the family of the Angevin kings of Sicily after the last heir of the Villehardouins departed in 1318. Quite different from the French princes, the Angevins of Sicily remained remote from the problems of Morea.[7] Battles against the Catalans of Attica and the Greeks dominate the period. The mercenary companies of Navarre established themselves in several parts of Morea after allying themselves with Nerio Acciajuoli and the Hospitalers.[8] After 1380 the principality was considerably diminished, almost to one-fourth of the Peloponnesus. Nerio Acciajuoli, a member of the Florentine family, became the master of Corinth, and another large part of the northern Peloponnesus was governed by the very powerful archbishop of Patras. The fortresses of Argos and Nafplion passed to Venice, which toward the end of the fourteenth century was showing a much greater interest in Morea because of the Turkish conquests of territories important to her commerce. She always retained Methone and Corone and was able to exercise some influence on Patras, whose archbishop, Paolo Foscari, was Venetian. Vostitsa belonged to the Narvarese, and the southeast Peloponnesus had belonged since 1382 to the Paleologues. One must also remember that all during the fourteenth century the Hospitalers tried to establish themselves in Morea and that the Turks were showing more and more audacity until finally in 1460 they became the sole masters of the Peninsula.

Venetian Romania: Crete, Euboea, Corfu, the Duchy of the Archipelagos

Venice had received half of the three-quarters of the empire during the partition of 1204, but she retained as a direct possession only Crete, which she bought from Boniface, together with Methone and Corone.[9] However, she kept a large part of Romania under her influence. In Morea, for example, Geoffrey and his successors had to become Venetian subjects, possess a respectable mansion in Venice, and consider themselves vassals of the doge. The Venetians remained exempt from payment of all customs in the principality, conducted commerce freely, and possessed in each town a church, a tribunal, and a storehouse.[10]

Under the Venetian administration, all of Crete and two small islands to the north were included in the kingdom of Candia. The kingdom of Negreponte was limited at first to the town of Chalkis or Negreponte (the rest of the island having been given to Lombard lords), and to the islands of Skyros and the Sporades to the north of Euboea. Venetian Romania also included the Venetian territory of Corfu and its dependencies on the coast of Epirus; and, on the neighboring islands; the region of Nafplion, Corone, and Methone and the protectorate of the Aegean islands[11] (map 3). Nevertheless, the kingdom of Candia was the most important of these possessions.

CRETE

The conquest of Crete proved the most difficult. The Genoese who were established on the island did not want to abandon it, while the Greeks violently opposed the new occupants and fought against the Venetians for several centuries. The Venetian Republic had to remain constantly alert for new upheavals of the Greek population.

After the Genoese left in 1208, Crete was placed under the authority of a Venetian duke. Giacomo Tiepolo, first (1208–16), submitted to the doge and the council a colonial military system capable of aiding in the policing of Crete and putting down local resistance. The system was adopted. Consequently the island was divided into three sorts of fiefs, conferred upon Venetian noblemen, rich Venetian merchants, and the clergy.[12] Crete was also divided into six provinces or sestiers, in accordance with the Venetian system, without regard to the rights of the big local proprietors.

The duke, governor of the island, was assigned for two years and resided in Candia. For its own benefit the commerce of Venice served the region of Candia to Fraschia as well as the territory around Temenos.[13] Venice was primarily concerned with establishing ports on the same plan as those of its own city and had little interest in the interior of Crete.

When the Venetian state and the Latin church were satisfied, the rest of the Cretan territory was divided among Venetian feudatories. Knighthoods were granted to 132 sons of the oldest Venetian families as soldiers of the *Serenissima*. Others coming from the Venetian populace received 48 lots as sergeants.

The new colonizers were primarily soldiers whose first duty was to protect the work of Venice. The feudatories had to defend trade so that the Venetian merchants could enjoy all the gains of their commerce. These merchants retained residences in Candia and had to act as docile auxiliaries to the Venetian civil authorities, who protected them and assured them of a privileged position. Thanks to this system, the Venetians retained Crete longer than any other Franks held territories, but in 1669 the Turks finally conquered the island.

EUBOEA

After the partition of the empire the island of Euboea was conquered by Boniface, king of Salonica; he divided it into three large fiefs, called *terzieri,* which he distributed to three of his companions, gentlemen from Verona. Rovano delle Carceri received the southern part of the island, with Carystos as its center; Giberto da Verona, the central part with Chalkis; and Pecorario dei Peicorari the north with Oreos.

Venice hastened to capitalize on the rights she had acquired on the island. In March 1209, a treaty established Venetian suzerainty over the *terzieri,* who from that time on owed homage to Venice, as did all the Latins and Greeks of Euboea. In this way the Venetian Republic obtained commercial privileges in all towns of Euboea. In 1216 she strengthened her hold over the island even more and broadened her action by installing a steward in Chalkis, charged with the administration of its interests. His jurisdiction soon extended over the whole island.[14] He acted in the name of the doge and of the commerce of Venice and had a variety of powers over the *terzieri.* The Venetian suzerainty over Euboea remained effective until the Turkish invasion, while in Morea it remained in effect in name only.

Corfu

The island of Corfu, which had been opened to Venetian commerce under the Byzantine Empire in 1198,[15] was one of the territories ceded to Venice upon the partition of the Latin Empire. Corfu belongs to the group of three islands, including Crete and Euboea, that Venice kept for herself. In 1207, ten Venetian lords were appointed to the administration of Corfu. In return they had to pay taxes to Venice, guarantee commercial privileges, and keep up the fortifications of the island. This agreement, however, was of short duration, for Michael I, despot of Greek Epirus and master of the Adriatic coast from Durazzo to Nafpactos, conquered Corfu and annexed it to his domain.

To retain it, in 1210 he recognized Venetian sovereignty over the island and over the ports he controlled on the Adriatic Sea. In 1267 the island changed hands, and for a century it was under the rule of the Anjou of Naples. In 1386 Venice reconquered Corfu and kept it for more than four centuries.

The Ionian islands of Cephalonia and Zante had been conquered in 1194 by Matteo Orsini of Apulia. When Venice occupied Corfu, Matteo temporarily recognized the overlordship of the Venetian Republic. Later, however, he pledged fidelity to William of Villehardouin, prince of Achaia, who conferred on him, in exchange, the title palatine count of Cephalonia. From 1479 to 1503, Cephalonia underwent a brief Turkish occupation, but it was later reoccupied by the Venetians, who kept it for three centuries.

THE DUCHY OF THE "ARCHIPELAGOS"

Most of the islands in the Aegean had been parceled out to Venice at the time of the partition. Since her resources were not great enough to conquer these islands and govern them, the republic decided to allow its citizens to occupy them. As a result, Marco Sanudo, nephew of the doge Dandolo, gathered a group of adventurers in eight galleys, and in 1207 he easily became master of the seventeen islands. He kept for himself the island of Naxos and distributed the rest as fiefs to his band of adventurers. The duchy of the Archipelagos, or Naxos, as it was alternatively called, lasted several centuries, until 1566, under the Sanudo and later the Crispi family. The island of Tenos remained under the Venetians even longer, until 1715.

The Islands of Cyprus, Rhodes, Chios, and Lesbos

The islands of Cyprus was almost untouched by the developments in the other Frankish territories. King Richard I of England conquered the island in 1191 during the Third Crusade, but he sold it almost immediately to the military order of the Templars. They found themselves too weak to govern it by themselves and sold it to Guy of Lusignan in 1192.

This first French lord organized the administration of the island according to the feudal code of Jerusalem, but he tried to retain a more centralized government by not dividing the island into fiefs and by giving fewer freedoms to the nobility.[16] Only toward the end of the fifteenth century, during the reign of Jacques II of Lusignan, can one detect Venetian influence on the Cypriot administration, through his Venetian wife, Caterina Cornaro. In 1489 Venice succeeded in occupying Cyprus and kept it until 1570, when the Turks conquered the island.[17]

RHODES

Rhodes was occupied by the Franks much later than the other Greek islands. At the time of the conquest of Constantinople Rhodes was in the hands of a very powerful Greek, Leon Gabalas, and so was never occupied by the Venetians as planned during the partition. But in 1309 Rhodes was conquered by the Hospitalers of the order of Saint John after they were expelled from Jerusalem by the Arabs at the end of the thirteenth century and took shelter in Cyprus. The Hospitalers also conquered the islands of Cos, Calymnos, Leros, Nisyros, Telos, Syme, Chalke, Icaria (after 1481), Delos, and Kastellorizon. Rhodes remained the center of their domain, and they governed these islands like feudal baronies.

Most of the grand masters, governors of Rhodes, were French, though the order was divided into eight tongues according to origins of the Hospitalers. The last governor was Philip of Villiers de l'Isle Adam; he courageously defended Rhodes against the Turks in 1522, but on 23 December he had to surrender it and seek refuge in Malta.

CHIOS AND LESBOS

The Genoese had not taken part in the Fourth Crusade; they nevertheless established themselves in the Aegean at the beginning of the fourteenth century. In this way the island of Chios was occupied in 1304–40 by a member of the Genoese family Zaccaria, whose name was Benedetto. In 1346 a private company whose members had adopted the name Giustiniani took over and governed it, as well as the islands of Icaria, Samos, and Psara; their government always remained under the direct control of Genoa. They remained in Chios until 1566.

The largest island, Lesbos (Mytilene), was part of the dowry of the sister of the Byzantine emperor John V, who married the Genoese Francesco I Gattilusio in 1355. Gattilusio's dynasty lasted until 1462. The Gattilusi were also the masters of the islands of Samothrace, Thassos, Lemnos, and Imbros.

Briefly stated, these were the political circumstances that shaped the development of the monastic and religious architecture of the Latin Middle Ages in Greece.

Part Two MONASTIC ARCHITECTURE

3 Architecture and the Cistercians

Soon after the fall of Constantinople, Innocent III approached the Emperor Baudouin about ways to attract large waves of immigration from the West to the new empire. It was especially to France, which had furnished the largest masses of Crusaders, that the pope and the emperor addressed themselves. In 1205 Innocent sent a letter to all the archbishops describing the riches of the Greek land and encouraging clergy and laymen to come and establish themselves in the new state. He also appealed to the religious orders of Western Europe to provide Latin brothers for the new land to compete for influence with the Greek monks.

But the European clergy did not demonstrate the enthusiasm the pope desired, and the immigrants were not numerous. Innocent thus had to rely primarily on the men who had taken part in the Crusade and in the conquest of the Latin Empire.

Among the first monastic orders to establish themselves in Greece were the Cistercians, who had also taken part in the Crusade.[1] During the first half of the thirteenth century they founded twelve monasteries (see Map 1).

Of these, two, or perhaps three, have survived the vicissitudes of the seven centuries since their founding. The most interesting is the ruined monastery of Zaraka, or Saracaz[2] as it was known in its own time, built by the Cistercians at the beginning of the thirteenth century. The others include the monastery of Isova, probably built by the Cistercians, and the monastery of Daphni, a former Byzantine monastery that was occupied by the Cistercians in the thirteenth century. The Latin monks of Daphni altered certain structures and made the necessary additions to their newly acquired establishment.

The Cistercians and Architecture

Cistercian churches in the West are easy to recognize. They are striking in their unity of form, as though built in the same spirit and resulting from a preestablished code. Art historians have commented at length about this architectural similarity and have often debated whether one can really speak of a Cistercian architectural style. Today this architectural unity is attributed to the personal influence of Saint Bernard and to the spirit of the order rather than to specific architectural rules laid down by the Cistercians for every detail of the buildings.[3]

The Cistercian church was conceived as a "workshop for prayer"[4] and thus in its ideal form was stripped of any nonessential artifice. Its main characteristic is the great simplicity and logic of all its elements. The plan terminates in a square apse and has a salient transept, in accordance with the Cistercian need for several altars distributed along the transept, rather than around a circular apse as at Cluny.

The sanctuary is simple and of modest dimensions. The vaults over the nave and the aisles never reach the height of those in the Benedictine churches. The interiors, with two-story elevations, as a rule have large windows without a passage at the base and retain excellent acoustics. Because of their reduced height and their aim of simplicitly, the Cistercian churches are, in general, poorly lit. They receive a limited amount of outside light yet are permitted only five candleholders in the interior. There is almost no sculptural ornamentation. The structural supports and the wall surfaces manifest a refusal to accept the richness of Cluniac decor. The austerity of the simple, smooth forms, lacking any kind of play, creates an imposing and monumental grandeur. In spite of its austere general appearance, Cistercian architecture is often surprising in its perfect proportions, its plasticity, and its very simple ornamental motifs.

Few Cistercian churches built before 1150 are extant: Fontenay, dated 1118, is one of the most ancient.[5] But one can find a similar approach in the architecture of Cistercian daughter houses all across Europe, often in areas remote from Burgundy, the cradle of the order.

The evolution of Cistercian forms had a considerable impact on the religious architecture of the Middle Ages. Although in some cases the forms changed very little, in other cases, and in certain regions, the spirit of the Cistercian buildings proved much more advanced than that of other ecclesiastical structures. The Cistercians adopted the ribbed vault of Burgundy, Champagne, and Ile de France after A.D. 1150 and carried it across Europe, thus helping spread the Gothic style. Though they adopted the ribbed vault, however, they never examined its possibilities, nor did they use it to modify the interior appearance of their churches. This is one of the reasons one can speak of Cistercian uniformity in architecture, for the Cistercian monks brought an unchanged manner of building to countries as distant as Greece.

The Establishment of New Monasteries

The founding of new Cistercian establishments was usually the result of too large a concentration of monks in one monastery. Generally the monks moved away twelve at a time at the invitation of a rich proprietor, a bishop or lord who wanted to establish Cistercians on his property or in his bishopric.[6] Less often they moved because they were given an existing monastery which had been inhabited by monks of another order.

The Cistercians never built their monasteries in towns. The rule of the order specifically forbade it: "In civitatibus, castellis villis nulla nostra construenda sunt coenobia."[7] In the West, in the early days of the order, the monks had a certain amount of liberty in choosing a site, though they could not establish themselves too close to another monastery. The statutes of 1153 demanded a distance of at least ten miles between abbeys. They also had to be remote from thoroughfares easily accessible to a large number of people. The Cistercians preferred valleys surrounded by wooded hills where there were springs.[8] The general plan of the monasteries and the disposition of the various buildings were very similar to the earlier monastic establishments (FIG. 1.) They conformed in that respect to the ancient monastic traditions that had also been observed by the Benedictines and the regular clergy.[9] Nevertheless, the Cistercians had difficulty adapting to monasteries built by other monks and preferred to construct their own buildings,[10] even if they had to wait several years. Outside France, however, they were often forced to settle in existing buildings. Such was the case in Spain at Sobrado and Valdedios, or in Greece at Daphni.

The Monastery of Zaraka

In a valley surrounded by high mountains near the Lake Stymphalia, remote even today from busy commercial roads, lie the ruins of the Cistercian monastery of Saracaz or Zaraka (PLATE 1).[11]

Fig. 1. *Traditional plan of a Cistercian monastery.*

Plate 1. Church of Zaraka. Ruins of the Cistercian monastery in the valley of Stymphalia. First quarter of the thirteenth century.

The date of construction of these monastic buildings is not certainly known. It is generally believed that they existed before 1236, for from that date until 1260 the monastery is mentioned in the pontifical correspondence and in the general chapters of the order.[12] Since the beginnings of the abbey are not specified in any of the documents, it is impossible to know with certainty from which monastery the monks of Zaraka developed.[13] We know only that before 1210 the prince of Morea (William of Champlitte) asked Pope Innocent III to send Cistercians from Hautecombe in Savoy to establish in Morea a monastery to which he would give some land. On 5 November 1210, Innocent III wrote to the abbot of the monastery of Hautecombe to ask him to send Anselmo, the Latin archbishop of Patras, the number of monks necessary for the new monastery.[14]

We also know that on another occasion Geoffrey I of Villehardouin asked the general chapter to send a group of monks to build a monastery in Achaia,[15] and that the chapter entrusted this task to the abbot of Morimond. We do not known what the chapter did after this decision, but it is probable that the monks settled in Andravida[16] or even Isova rather than Zaraka. Fortunately, the archeological excavations of 1924–30, undertaken by the Archeological Society under the direction of A. Orlandos, and the later excavations by E. Stikas in 1962, give a fairly clear idea of the plan of the church and a more general idea of the location of the other buildings, which today are completely in ruins. There is not a single ancient description of them such as frequently exist for destroyed monuments.[17]

DESCRIPTION OF THE CHURCH

The plan. The plan of the church of Zaraka, as it can be reconstructed from its ruined remains, indicates that it was the filial of Clairvaux (FIG. 2). This is so especially because of its flat eastern end, which follows the plan of Saint Bernard as we know it,[18] although, as I mentioned, Cistercian architecture has no model characteristics (PLATE 2).[19]

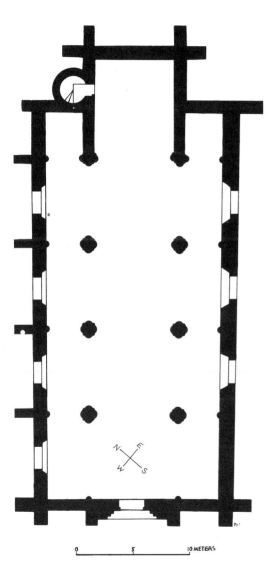

Fig. 2. *The Cistercian church of Zaraka. Built before* A.D. *1236. Plan of the church.*

Plate 2. *Zaraka. View of the sanctuary.*

The plan of the church of Zaraka is rectangular, with a nave and two aisles, no transept, and a square choir flanked by two square chapels. As a result, it has only straight lines, which intercept at 90° angles. The nave and aisles each have four bays. Those of the nave are square, the others are rectangular (PLATE 3).

Plate 3. Zaraka. View from the northwest.

The width of the church varies from 15.50 m at the western entrance to 15.80 m in front of the choir. The dimensions are modest, as in most Cistercian churches. The length of the exterior walls reaches almost 34 m and the sanctuary wall extends another 4.30 m from the chapels. The church is oriented southwest to northeast.

The northern exterior angle of the sanctuary encompasses a small circular tower with a round staircase. Orlandos speculates in his plan that this was the bell tower of the church.[20] Stone bell towers had been strictly forbidden by the general chapter in 1157.[21] The rule limited bells to 500 pounds, so that one man could ring them. In 1274, quite exceptionally, the chapter accepted a stone bell tower, but only in a place where powerful winds had destroyed wooden towers. The rule was usually respected in France and Germany but much less in Spain, Italy, and England, where towers over the central part of the church were used.[22] This could have also been true in Greece, as in Zaraka.

The interior space of the church is divided by two rows of five piers with four engaged shafts at the corners (PLATE 4). Two of these piers in each row, at the eastern and western ends of the nave, are engaged in the wall. The piers at the eastern end finish off the projecting wall that separates the sanctuary from the adjoining chapels (FIG. 2). The four bays of the nave are twice as wide as the corresponding bays of the aisles and divide the interior of the church into four equal parts. The older practice of building a wide nave had been achieved in Romanesque churches by groin or barrel vaulting and was often retained by Cistercian churches, reducing the aisles to mere passages.[23] The sanctuary formed an extension of the central nave and had the dimension of one of its bays, while the area of the square chapels at the ends of the aisles was only one-fourth that of the sanctuary.

Plate 4. Zaraka. Interior space looking west.

The church of Zaraka had no narthex, unlike most Cistercian churches. It was completely covered with rib vaults, a method the Cistercians were among the first to adopt and to spread all over Europe (PLATE 5).

The vaults of the aisles seem to have been approximately 5.50m from the ground, but it is impossible to estimate the height of the nave, for not enough of the church remains standing to warrant any hypothesis.[24]

According to Orlandos, there could not have been a triforium between the two stories.[25] An arcade separated the central nave from the aisles. Above it there must have been large clerestory windows to light the nave (FIG. 3).

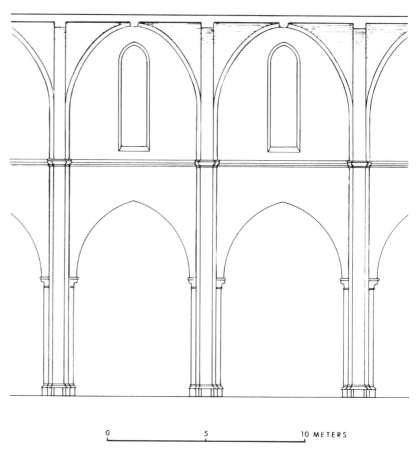

Fig. 3. *The Cistercian church of Zaraka. Proposed restoration of the elevation.*

0   5   10 METERS

Plate 5. Zaraka. Part of a rib.

The two-story elevation was certainly characteristic of Cistercian architecture, which forbade excessive height over the aisles and maintained the balanced proportions of 2:1 that suggested an atmosphere of humility.[26] This practice became common in Europe from the second half of the thirteenth century, not only in Cistercian architecture but in many other religious buildings.

The arcades of the church of Zaraka dividing the nave and aisles were carried by piers with four engaged columns that supported the rib vaults of the roof (FIG. 4). These piers were formed by a central round core 1.28 m in diameter, with four engaged half-columns 0.175 m in diameter (PLATE 6). The whole pier rested on a low polygonal base 0.30 m in height. The half-columns were placed where they could receive the diagonal ribs of the vault. The general form of these piers is that found in France in the first half of the thirteenth century.[27]

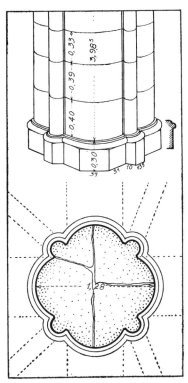

Fig. 4. *Reconstruction of the church of Zaraka by Orlandos. Attached pillars.*

Plate 6. *Zaraka. Pier with engaged colonnette.*

Exactly opposite the piers along the northern and southern walls are the remnants of engaged columns, flanked by two colonnettes that together with the piers of the nave carried the ribbed vaults. These columns and colonnettes had only one trapezoidal capital, whose angles were concealed by leaves forming volutes and a cross in the center (PLATE 7). Each was surmounted by a molded abacus. The sculptural ornamentation is very simple, as the Cistercians usually preferred, for their utilitarian architecture served a role precisely defined by the rule of the order.[28] In spite of the scarcity of ornamentation there is a sense of beauty owing to the clarity of masses and the perfection of execution.

Plate 8. *Zaraka. Base of a pier dividing the nave from the aisles.*

Plate 7. *Zaraka. Engaged column and capital in the southern wall.*

The capitals of Zaraka resemble those of the chapter house of the Cistercian monastery of Silvacane in southern France, built between 1175 and 1230. This method of depicting simple leaves in the form of volutes at the angles of capitals can be found from Fontenay to Pontigny, as well as in Italy at Chiara-valle di Catagnola, built at the end of the twelfth century.[29] Despite their simplicity, the capitals are distinguished by a plasticity characteristic of Gothic capitals at the beginning of the thirteenth century.

The engaged piers between the choir and the chapels had a less symmetrical form, being more elongated and equaling only three-quarters of the free-standing piers (PLATE 8).[30] In the four corners of the church stood simple shafts that carried the vaults. One can still see the capital in place at the western angle of the northern aisle (PLATES 9 and 10).

The bases of the piers are not all of the same form. The piers with the four engaged half-columns at the corners have polygonal plinths 0.30 m high, topped by a molding; the engaged columns in the side walls and the shafts placed at the angles of the chapel and the choir have rectangular bases of different heights, from 0.64 m to 0.315 m, on which the shafts are carried.[31] The taller ones are at the angles of the choir. These differences were most likely due to the unevenness of the ground, and it is possible that the choir and the chapels were raised slightly above the nave and aisles.

Plate 10. Zaraka. Engaged column in the southern aisle.

Plate 9. Zaraka. Capital of an engaged column in the western corner of the northern aisle.

The piers with four engaged half-columns at the corners, the engaged columns in the walls of the aisles, and the corner shafts all suggest that the church was entirely covered with ribbed vaults. Several fragments of ribs with a rather heavy and simple profile were exposed during the archeological digs, along with more capitals (PLATES 11 and 12). Also, two keystones were unearthed. One is sculpted in the shape of a rosette; the other has a human face surrounded by leaves (PLATE 13). More evidence of a vaulted roof can be found in the walls; for example, on the southern wall it is still possible to see that the piers carried arches. The vaults over the aisles must have been approximately 5.50m in height, which is also the height of the exterior buttresses (FIG. 5).

Plate 11. Zaraka. Capital with foliage.

Plate 12. Zaraka. Capital with volutes.

There is no doubt that the ribs of the rib vaults of the aisles were carried by the engaged half-columns of the piers, while the transverse arches rested on the polygonal imposts of the capital.[32]

Fig. 5. Reconstruction of the church of Zaraka
by Orlandos.

Plate 13. Zaraka, keystone with human face.
Compare drawing by Villard de Honnecourt.

Because of the ruined condition of the upper parts of the building,
it is not possible to know the exact height of the ceiling of the nave
or the appearance of the elevation of the church.[33] The engaged
half-columns of the piers probably continued up to the clerestory
windows, where they met the ribs of the vault, very similar to the
transept of the abbey of Fontfroide. The vaults of the nave were
probably not placed very high, for until the thirteenth century the
Cistercian semi-Gothic often retained low vaults and thick walls
reinforced by powerful buttresses.

The exterior of the church of Zaraka, except for the buttresses,
resembles in plan an early Cistercian basilica, with its almost
rectangular plan and its lack of transept (PLATE 15). The vaults of
the aisles, as well as the wall of the eastern sanctuary and the
northern and western walls, were supported by massive vertical
rectangular buttresses, 1.60 m at their bases but tapering off gradually at the top (PLATE 14). The sanctuary had four buttresses, two
at each corner of its square end, which formed extensions of the
walls. The southern wall was probably oriented toward the cloister

and had no buttresses, but it was much thicker than the northern wall, 1.39 m as against 0.99 m.

Plate 14. Zaraka. Exterior view of the northern wall with its buttresses.

Plate 15. Zaraka. General view from the north-west.

The western facade had buttresses at the angles and on both sides of the central portal in the same axis as the interior colonnades of the nave (PLATE 16).

The exterior wall is 1 m thick except in the center of the western facade, where there is a portal and the wall has been thickened to 1.72 m. This portal had a projecting gable that abutted on the two central buttresses. In both sides of the door, whose opening is 2.20 m, there are three colonnettes whose bases probably carried voussoirs in the form of pointed arches (FIG. 5). The bases of these colonnettes are not very high and are composed of flattened tori placed on plinths.

The walls between the corner buttresses and the central door are bare. Two small colonnettes that rise at the angles of the buttresses probably supported blind arcades. One can draw a parallel between this portal and the one in the Cistercian abbey church of Fossanova in Italy.[34] Several parts of the sculptural decor of the facade of Zaraka have been found. One can still see the base of the northwestern colonnettes placed between the buttress and the wall and its capital with floral decorations. At the southern angle of the portal there still remains a capital with acanthus leaves (PLATE 17).

Plate 16. Zaraka. Western facade.

According to Orlandos's reconstruction (FIG. 5), one can visualize a facade of great simplicity and formal beauty, where the massive wall contrasts with the rare and delicate sculpture of the capitals and voussoirs. One immediately recognizes the typical characteristics of Cistercian art: deeply rooted in Romanesque art, it nevertheless distinguishes itself by its anti-Romanesque and rationalistic spirit.

Two other doors on the southeastern side of the church open onto the cloister. They were unearthed during the excavations of 1962. Another door led from the sanctuary to the bell tower.

The church was lit by rather large windows at the floor level and, according to Orlandos's reconstruction, with smaller ones at the clerestory level over the nave. No windows have been found in place, but many fragments were scattered among the ruins (PLATE 18). One can also still see the site of each window on the northwestern side, at a height of 3.10m, and in the three first bays. There must have been four windows on the north side and three on the south side facing the cloister (PLATE 19). One the south side, large openings in the ruins prevent a clear view of their exact location (PLATE 20). The condition of the eastern wall permits no speculation on the number or shape of the windows that lit the choir.

Plate 17. Zaraka. Ruined capital engaged in the northwest corner.

Plate 18. Zaraka. Section of the tracery of a window.

The aisle windows were in the Gothic style of the second quarter of the thirteenth century, which led to the Rayonnant style of a few years later: two lights crowned by pointed arches, surmounted by an oculus designed in fine bar tracery (FIG. 6). From 1220 on, windows like these appeared first at the cathedral of Reims in the radiating chapels and a little later in the nave over the aisles of Amiens.[35] This indicates that the church of Zaraka certainly could not have been finished before 1225.[36] It is impossible to know exactly what the clerestory windows looked like. There is no proof that they were single-light windows as Orlandos has represented them in his reconstruction.

The nave was probably also lit by a window on the western facade (FIG. 5). Since there never were stained-glass windows in Cistercian churches, there must have been none at Zaraka. Rubble masonry and reused ancient stones formed the greatest part of the walls, the largest being placed at the base of the walls and at the angles. Higher up, the rubble and brick were drowned in mortar in a very irregular manner. The whole wall was then faced with well-cut ashlar placed regularly in horizontal bands. Though all the walls were made of

Plate 19. Zaraka. Detail of the interior of a window in the southern wall.

Plate 20. Zaraka. Southern wall, interior view.

the same materials, they do not have the same appearance everywhere. As already mentioned, the southern wall was much thicker and without buttresses.

The surrounding monastic buildings of the abbey. The cloister must have been situated against this southern wall. A roof inclined toward the courtyard covered the gallery of the cloister and was carried on corbels that can still be seen projecting from the wall of the church. Two doors led from the church to the cloister. There are no remains of the other buildings that existed on the southern and eastern sides of the church.

Surrounding all the buildings there must have been a protective wall, of which only the entrance gate remains. One still can see a square tower 7.40 m × 7.80 m that was used as a bastion. On the ground level one passes under a barrel vault reinforced by a transverse arch. The enceinte must have abutted exactly at that point of the tower, for one can still see its traces. (PLATE 21). The upper part of the tower is in very poor condition, and the masonry is less carefully done than that of the church. Cistercian monks generally built their abbeys by themselves with the help of converts and a master builder, usually a monk, following the plan of the mother

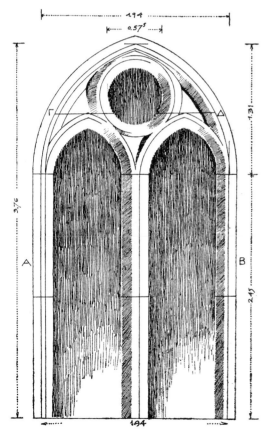

Fig. 6. Window of the church of Zaraka. Drawing by A. Orlandos.

Plate 21. Zaraka. Ruined entrance tower, western view.

abbey. Often they could not erect all the building of their monastery at once. They started with the chuch and raised temporary buildings for their living quarters. At Zaraka, the monks doubtless built the church themselves. They were probably helped by Greek converts or workers from the local population, but the church of Zaraka is purely Western architecture. We are of course deprived of a great many informative details, but from the bar tracery of the windows it does not seem probable that the church of Zaraka was built before 1224. It must have been outstanding for its simplicity and clear forms and for the contrast of its massive walls with the delicate sculptural decor of the capitals, bar tracery, and voussoirs.

The Monastery of Isova

One other Cistercian monastery is extant in the Peloponnesus: the monastery of Our Lady of Isova. When Jean Buchon visited the monastery of Isova in Gortynia in the nineteenth century, he labeled it Benedictine. He was as much surprised as the travelers who had preceded him to find Gothic forms in a country so remote from France.[37] His description corresponds very well to the impression the monastery still gives today: "A little above a fountain of excellent water," he writes, rise "vast ruins of two buildings." One was a vast Latin church; the walls are almost entirely preserved, and one finds all the forms of Gothic churches, with large windows surrounded by pointed arches.[38] He continues, "The spot was deliciously well chosen in the midst of a forest on a softly inclined hill down to the Alpheus and to a smaller river, the Tsemberagon or Dragon. This environment reminded me of that of the Benedictine monastery of la Cava. The Benedictines always chose admirably the spot of their monasteries and in examining these ruins my memories carried me to some old monasteries in France and England" (PLATE 22).[39]

Since Buchon's time the monastery of Isova had always been accepted as a Benedictine monastery, with no real justification except the lack of information to attribute it to another order.[40] Our Lady of Isova, the name given to the large building, is mentioned several times in the Chronicle of Morea, and we thus know positively that it was destroyed in 1263 during the battle of Prinitsa, when Turkish mercenaries in the service of the Greeks burned it.[41]

Next to the church of Our Lady of Isova rises the second building mentioned by Buchon, the Chapel of Saint Nicolas. Equally ruined, it is of slightly later date.

Plate 22. Our Lady of Isova. Early thirteenth century.

THE CHURCH OF OUR LADY OF ISOVA

The plan of the church of Our Lady forms a long rectangle with a single nave of 41.30 m × 15.20 m not including the extensions of the buttresses at the southwest angle, which extends to the west and to the south. To the east, there is a shallow five-sided polygonal apse 9.60 m long and 8.20 m wide (FIG. 7). The western side (PLATE 23) and the northern wall (PLATE 24) have remained almost undisturbed, in contrast to the southern wall, which is badly shattered, and the apse, which is completely destroyed. The single nave of the church is impressive because of its large size: 38.45 m × 12.50 m. The walls are 1.37 m thick, whereas the choir walls are only 0.80 m thick and are reinforced by six buttresses, placed at intervals of approximately 3.60 m.

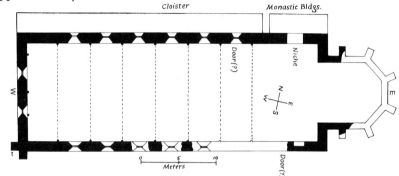

Fig. 7. Our Lady of Isova (Cistercian?). Destroyed in A.D. *1263. Plan of the church.*

Plate 23. Our Lady of Isova. Western facade, interior view.

Plate 24. Our Lady of Isova. Northern view.

The interior of Our Lady of Isova shows no traces of dividing columns or pillars, leading to the assumption that it had a single nave covered by a wooden inclined roof that rested on light stone corbels regularly spaced along the walls between the windows (PLATE 25). They are 4.50 m from today's floor level but, it is impossible to know their exact height without excavation, since the ground is now cluttered with weeds, trees, and dirt. The northern wall rises 7.50 m above this heap of accumulated rubbish.

Plate 25. Our Lady of Isova. Interior view of the windows of the northern wall.

The corbels carrying the roof are spaced 4.10m to 4.40m. A greater number exist on the northern wall than on the southern, which suffered greater damage from the fire. The walls and the corbels retain a slight pinkish stain, which proves that the fire mentioned in the Chronicle damaged this section. The last corbel to the east on the southern wall retains certain sculptured decorations.

The walls, made of pieces of well-cut sandstone fitted into mortar, with occasional pieces of brick, give the impression of neat workmanship. The blocks used at the angles of the building, on the frames of the windows, and on the cornices and gutters are also of well-cut sandstone and good-quality tufa. The walls retain square holes left by the scaffolding, not filled for lack of time (PLATE 24). It seems evident that all the walls were erected by the Latin monks without interruption. The construction is plain, however, with no trace of ornamentation and no influence by Byzantine craftsmanship.[42]

On the northern and southern sides, over a projecting stone girdle about 4 m from today's ground level, were six windows, concentrated toward the center of the building (PLATE 18). In the first bay to the west and the two last bays before the choir, the wall had no windows. The six were narrow, one-light lancet windows, with a larger embrasure on the inner side than on the outer, and with a pointed arch coming to a joint rather than locked in by a keystone (PLATE 25). The projecting stone band stops before the end of the wall to the west, where another building must have leaned on the wall itself.

The western facade was divided into three bays by three pointed arches. The two lower arches are also narrower measuring 0.67 m × 2.40 m, as against the higher one, which is 1.20 m × 3.60 m (PLATE 19). Very little is left of the eastern polygonal apse, and it is extremely difficult to know the exact location of the windows. Traquair, who saw it earlier in this century when it was in slightly better condition, suggested that there were three windows of about 1 m width, with two lights of the type also found at Zaraka, but whose tracery forms at the top a rose with five petals, resting on two pointed arches. Such windows, also described at Zaraka, appear first in the Champagne and a little later, between 1220 and 1230, in the Ile de France.

Traquair reconstructed the shape of these windows from a stone molding that constituted a fragment of the tracery of one of the windows, reused at a later date in the construction of a nearby road fountain (PLATE 26).[43] From this fragment he suggested that the tracery of the rose window was glazed. This is very doubtful, however. In the state of the building today, it is also impossible to accept his statement that the window with the two lights, as well as the rest of the windows of the church, was protected by iron bars because of the holes still visible in the wall.

On the western side the church had no doors, contrary to Buchon's belief.[44] It is most probable that there was a door on the southeastern part, where today there is a large opening. To the east of this opening the wall has a concave molding that suggests the presence of a door.

Plate 26. Our Lady of Isova. Arch built over a fountain.

Traquair's plan suggests another door on the northwestern side, communicating with the cloister on that side. Today one can see three openings on that side, one of which very probably was a door (PLATE 24). It must have been indispensable for the monks to communicate directly with the church from the side of the cloister.[45] The ground level certainly must have been much lower at that time to accommodate a door with a pointed arch.

Of the two openings on the northern side, the hardest to explain convincingly is the middle one. One could perhaps imagine a door communicating with the gallery of the cloister, but there is no proof for such a hypothesis. The third opening in the last eastern bay was a niche, which today is completely destroyed. Only one part of it is left, on the right side. One can still see a capital placed on a corner colonnette, whose floral decorations are hard to distinguish.

Another niche was placed right across from it on the southern side, framed by a pointed arch with a molding and decorated with nine small flowers in relief, rather delicately executed (PLATE 27). Over the niche, according to Traquair, were two trilobe arcades surmounted by a quatrefoil.[46] Unfortunately, the corner colonnettes of the niche on which the arch rested have disappeared. The niche was probably used as a font.

Plate 27. Our Lady of Isova. Niche in the southern wall.

The single nave of Our Lady was certainly covered by a pointed wooden roof. The sharp gable of the western facade and the corbels placed between the windows on the southern and northern sides to support it are proof enough of this. In the present state of ruin, we cannot be sure whether the gable was higher than the roof or whether the roof rested on it. Most probably the gable was placed under the roof (PLATE 28).[47] It is also difficult to explain why the corbels were placed so low on the wall and exactly how the roof was supported by them.

The width of the single nave was not excessive, and there was no need for intermediate supports. The wooden roof supported by beams did not require buttresses. On the northern side, the church leans toward the cloister, and only two vertical buttresses topped by cornices supported the southwestern corner. Over the first cornice the western wall protrudes sharply and is supported at its base by a corbel in the form of a trefoil. Further up the northern wall at the level of the cornice, the angle ends in a salient block decorated by a human face, which probably served as a drain (PLATE 29).[48] The polygonal apse of Our Lady of Isova must have been covered by a ribbed vault. Although no part of the roof is standing today, since

Plate 28. *Our Lady of Isova. Western facade.*

Plate 29. *Our Lady of Isova. Southwestern corner.*

it suffered the greatest destruction, a rib of its vault was found incorporated into the wall of the neighboring church of Saint Nicolas, which must have come from the apse of Our Lady. Its profile is more complex than those of the ribs found in Morea.[49]

THE OTHER MONASTIC BUILDINGS

Cistercian abbeys strictly follow the rules about the placement and distribution of their buildings, except in extreme cases where the formation of the landscape obliged the monks to make certain modifications. At Isova the cloister and the other buildings were placed to the north of the church where the ground was flatter rather than on the southern side where it was more steeply inclined, even though cloisters were traditionally placed on the south. As was customary, the monks had placed the church on the highest part of the hill and the cloister on the most level land. One also finds this distribution of buildings in the Cistercian abbeys of Font-froide, Pontigny, Floran, Silvacane in France and Tintern in Wales. At OurLady of Isova, the cloister was placed all along the north wall of the church. One can still see two lines of corbels placed one over the other (PLATE 30). The twelve upper corbels, 3m above today's ground level, held the wooden roof of the gallery of the cloister exactly under the window of the church. The second row of eight corbels is aligned 2.20m under the first row, between the two openings in the church wall that must have served as doors providing access from the church to the cloister. The corbels supported a wooden floor laid some distance above the ground, under which one could probably enter. Today this is not possible because the ground is much higher than it was in the thirteenth century.[50] The same gallery continued on the western side. On the eastern side, at a right angle to the church, the foundations of a building can be seen. It probably had two floors and was 8.65m wide. One can still detect traces on the church walls of the pointed roof and of the supports that held the wooden floor of the second story.[51] This part of the ruins of Isova again bears striking similarity to the Cistercian Abbey of Tintern.

The second story was used, it seems, as a dormitory for the monks. There is unfortunately no indication of the location of the refectory, nor is there any clue to the nature of the other buildings to the north, since there are no remnants. There is also no information about the existence of a wall surrounding these buildings.

Plate 30. Our Lady of Isova. Corbels on the exterior of the northern wall.

THE FOUNDATION OF THE MONASTERY

The lack of information on the construction and date of founding of Our Lady makes it impossible to do more than place it according to its architectural style in a certain period and region of Western monastic architecture. Lavedan stated that "there are two categories of architects, those who conceive a building as a plan, that is as a play of lines and those who conceive of it as a game of volume, not to mention those who only see in it a pretext for decoration."[52] By this standard the builders of Our Lady were interested only in the plan and kept the volumes and decoration as simple as possible. It is from this plan, then, that one must determine what monks built Our Lady of Isova and exactly when in the first half of the thirteenth century they constructed it.

The task is difficult, especially because of the simplicity of the plan. This very simplicity, added to the lack of decorative elements, obliges us to put aside any suggestion that it was a Benedictine monastery. After all, no historical document encourages such a supposition. On the contrary, we know that there were at least two Cistercian foundations in the region of Achaia, whose exact location we do not know. The first was established after Geoffrey of Villehardouin approached the pope in 1210 at the suggestion of the archbishop Anselme.[53] He wanted monks of Hautecombe to establish a monastery in Morea.[54] According to Clair, they settled in Zaraka. The second was established after 1225, when Geoffrey presented a second request to the Cistercian general chapter for another Cistercian monastery. The abbey of Morimond undertook to send the monks.[55] We know positively, however, of only one Cistercian monastery, the one at Zaraka, though there were two in Morea during the first quarter of the thirteenth century. It is, then, very probable that Our Lady of Isova was a Cistercian monastery.

Churches with a single nave were not uncommon in the West. They are characteristic of modest Gothic buildings found in the thirteenth century in southern France and Catalonia. Some are vaulted and others, even simpler, are covered by pointed wooden roofs. This plan had been profusely spread across France in the Romanesque period and is found among the more massive and heavy structures. Documents speak of the single nave of the first Cistercian church in 1105. The complete disappearance of southern buildings of the twelfth century and the absence of written descriptions like those relating to Burgundy allows us to cite no examples except perhaps for the Cistercian church of Sylvanes, built in 1151–87, which is still in existence.

From the end of the twelfth century and the thirteenth century one can cite Bonnecombe and Beaulieu, daughters of Clairvaux. In Spain the Cistercian church of Bonifeza, established in 1235, has a polygonal apse like that of Our Lady of Isova, but differs in being completely vaulted. Other examples are Bugedo de Juarros near Burgos and in Sicily Saint Nicholas of Girgenti.[56] In Syria the Cistercian church of Belmont from the end of the twelfth century also has only one nave.[57] In the thirteenth century this single nave becomes characteristic of the Mediterranean regions rather than just of Cistercian churches.

The mendicant orders, Dominicans and Franciscans, whose role was to mingle with the people, preferred this plan and spread it even more widely than the Cistercians. In Isova, however, it seems quite improbable that the church of Our Lady and its monastery were built by the latter orders, even though the plan might encourage such a hypothesis. Our Lady is situated much too far from a community, which was so necessary for the Franciscan and Dominican fathers. The absence of a portal on the western side indicates even more strongly that the monks of Isova lived cloistered in an atmosphere of contemplation.

The single nave had been the rule for the Cistercian nunneries.[58] One can mention as examples the churches of Droiteval in the Vosges and of Bouchet near Valence from the twelfth century; of Beauvoir near Bourges of 1234; of Vignogoul and Gigean, both near Montpellier, of 1250, as well as Saint Loup near Orleans, from the end of the thirteenth century. Fille Dieu in Switzerland and Lieu in the Haute Savoie, built in the fourteenth century, should also be added to this category. Very few of these churches were vaulted, and many had polygonal apses.

In Morea we know there was a monastery of Cistercian nuns at Methone dedicated to Santa Maria de Verge and that in 1267 the nuns were forced by the Greeks to leave for Italy.[59] But it is improbable that Our Lady of Isova was inhabited by nuns, for it was too far from a town and was completely unprotected. Its plan, though, corresponds closely to the examples already mentioned.

The pointed wooden roof of Our Lady of Isova most definitely stems from Western practice. The Greek buildings, even the simplest and poorest, never used such a method of roofing. For this reason it is inconceivable that the church of Isova was influenced by local habits. The roof is also not characteristic of Benedictine churches, where there is a subtler play of volume. On the contrary, the rule of the Cistercian order prescribed the same height over almost the whole church. To Saint Bernard, the height of Cluniac buildings and the inequality between the main nave and aisles appeared as vanity, hardly a Christian characteristic.[60]

Pointed wooden roofs were well known, indeed customary, not only in the Romanesque period but also in the thirteenth and fourteenth centuries.[61] They were characteristic in both the north and the south of France, as at Lamourguier in Narbonne, whose church dates from the thirteenth century.[62]

To the south of the Pyrenees this type of roof was even more popular, especially in Catalonia. One finds it on almost all monastic churches.[63] It was also characteristic of certain other buildings, like the Cistercian dormitory of Santa Cruz (1191), the refectory of the Cistercian abbey of Fossanova (1187–1208), or the infirmary of Casamari of about 1200.[64] These roofs are often placed on pointed arches built in stone or on diaphragm arches, though no remnants of such arches exist at Isova.[65] We must still keep in mind that the corbels between the windows are placed too low to have supported the roof directly.

Although we have no proof of the origin of the monks who built Our Lady of Isova, it seems very probable that we owe these structures to the Cistercians that Geoffrey of Villehardouin requested in 1225. The Cistercian buildings often, of course, vary in their plans and structural detail, but they all retain a family air that also characterizes Our Lady of Isova. The ampleness of the single nave, the polygonal apse, and the pointed wooden roof all relate it to the south of France[66] or to Italy rather than to Burgundy, and perhaps the monks that built it came from the daughter house of Morimond.[67] The style of the windows of Our Lady places it about 1225.

Innocent III had on many occasions expressed his interest in the Cistercians through contact and through them he hoped to gradually persuade the Byzantine clergy to show some esteem for the clergy of the West. According to Innocent, the severity of their discipline and the sanctity of their life could not fail to favorably influence the Greeks, who had always held solitary monks in great respect.[68]

SAINT NICOLAS OF ISOVA: DESCRIPTION

Approximately 20m from the church of Our Lady, on the southern side, rises the church of Saint Nicolas, built after 1263 when a fire destroyed the monastery (PLATE 31). The plan of Saint Nicolas forms a rectangle 10.95m wide and 9.70m long. The church's east side ends in a projecting semicircular apse flanked by two shallow semi-circular chapels inscribed in the straight exterior wall.

Plate 31. Saint Nicolas of Isova. The sanctuary seen next to Our Lady of Isova.

The interior of the church consists of a nave and two aisles separated by two pairs of arches resting on two columns, whose square bases, 0.80m in width, still exist (FIG. 8). These arches were supported on the east and west sides by pilasters engaged in the walls, of which one can see traces over the imposts. Exactly under these, the bases can still be seen in their original places.

There is no trace of an iconostasis. The bases of the central columns are formed by a square plinth on which rests an attic base whose forms extend as far out as the plinth. At the angles, leaves are carved into the soft tufa in a naturalistic manner, reminiscent of thirteenth-century Western patterns.[69] Their Western appearance suggests that these bases may have been transferred from the monastery of Isova after the fire. In the church of Our Lady, however, there is no indication of where they could have come from.

The nave of Saint Nicolas was higher than the side aisles. It had a two-story elevation, according to Traquair, who attempted a reconstruction based on the ruins. These are better preserved on the eastern and western sides of the church. The arcades that separate the nave from the aisles must have had pointed arches in the same manner as the windows (FIG. 8).[70] Over each arch was a small clerestory window that allowed light to enter the nave. The upper part of the nave was at the same level as the gable pierced by a window on the west side.

The eastern end had three lancet windows protected by iron bars, whose place is still visible (PLATE 32). The pointed arches over these narrow windows were carved out of the same block or formed by two stones.

Plate 32. *Saint Nicolas of Isova. Eastern end.*

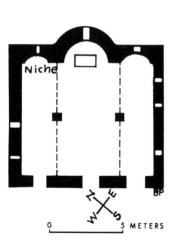

Fig. 8. *Saint Nicolas of Isova. Build after* A.D. *1263. Plan of the church.*

The windows of the projecting apse were larger (1.03 m) and had two lights, separated by a central colonnette. In the wall is a large opening. West of it is an entire window and to the east a fragment of another. On the interior of this wall there is one niche, while the north wall has several: one in the northwest corner, one in the center of the wall with a pointed arch,[71] and still another three toward the eastern part of the wall, the middle one larger than the two others. All three were placed over a "piscina" with six lobes (PLATE 33).

Higher up on the same wall were three windows with pointed arches, the one in the northwest bay larger than the others. Among the niches on the northern side was a small door with a straight lintel.[72] From the western facade one enters the church through three doors that led directly into the three naves through a narthex or porch. It is not possible to know whether there was also a door on the southern side, for today there is a large opening in the wall.

The walls, 0.82 m thick, are made of rectangular pieces of ashlar with pieces of brick and tile. They are less regularly constructed than those of Our Lady of Isova. The bricks and tiles frame the stones, forming a design in the masonry. A molded cornice runs along the northern and southern walls of the aisles and continues on the eastern wall, crowning the apse exactly under the semidome.

The moldings of this cornice consist of a torus between two fillets, and end at the bottom in a larger curved band.[73] One part of a rib from the vault of the choir of Our Lady was found imbedded in the masonry, proving that Saint Nicolas was built after the destruction of the church of Our Lady.[74] The covering of Saint Nicolas was like that of Our Lady, a pointed wooden roof, but it offered a very different aesthetic appearance, for it was placed higher up and resembled the roofs of simple early Christian basilicas. The aisles were covered by inclined roofs, and the apse had a half dome. The plan of Saint Nicolas contains nothing that recalls the plans of Western churches, but as noted before this basilical plan of three naves separated by two columns is also absent from Byzantine architecture.[75]

The church of Saint Nicolas must have been built by Latin monks, but certainly not by Cistercians, since the only known monastery of this order on the Greek peninsula after 1276 was the one at Daphni.

From the style of Saint Nicolas, it is impossible to guess the origin of the new inhabitants. It is clear that the church of Our Lady was built by the monks themselves, probably helped by a few local workers, as was customary with the Cistercians. Saint Nicolas, on the contrary, must have been built primarily by Greek workers. It is possible that the monks who came to settle at Isova after the larger church was burned were not as numerous and had to depend on the Greek population for the construction of their church. Naturally these workers applied the forms they used in their own constructions. The square plan and the semicircular apse, the win-

Plate 33. Saint Nicolas of Isova. Niche with a pointed arch in the northern wall.

dow embrasures with straight wooden lintels, and the masonry mixed with brick recall Greek structures. In contrast, the basilican plan, the lack of narthex and iconostasis, the pointed arches, the bases of the columns, and the capitals are of Western inspiration.

According to Traquair, Saint Nicolas must have been built during the fifteenth century. He sees a relationship between Saint Nicolas and Saint Sozomena, a Latin church in Cyprus mentioned by Enlart, which is of the same period.[76] But this similarity is very general and not very convincing. On the contrary, it is much more probable that the monks established themselves in Isova in the second half of the thirteenth century, certainly after 1263[77] and not very long after the fire and the departure of the monks who had built the church of Our Lady. It is probable that the new monks were southern Italians and had come to Morea during the Angevin rule. They were no doubt more willing to accept certain Byzantine habits in construction than were the French from Burgundy or the Midi.[78]

The Monastery of Daphni

Daphni, on the road from Eleusis to Athens, remains one of the most beautiful, most ancient, and most important Byzantine monasteries of Attica. It existed as early as the fifth century and most probably was built on the site of a sanctuary of Apollo[79] that was destroyed by Alaric. The church of the older monastery was a basilica, surrounded by an almost square fortified outer wall built of large ashlar stones, approximately 100m on each side. Its entrance was on the west between two large bastions. With its projecting square towers, it resembled the military constructions of Justinian.[80] The ruins of this wall are extant.

The present church, built to the east of the original basilica, is more recent and is differently oriented to the outer wall. This second church was built at the end of the eleventh century[81] and dedicated to the Virgin of Vlachernes. Its plan is a cross inscribed in a rectangle, surmounted by an octagonal dome. It had a narthex and an open porch over which a second story had been built, probably housing a library and the private apartments of the abbot (FIG. 9).[82]

On the arrival of the Franks, the Greek monks had to abandon the monastery, which had fallen into the hands of the Crusaders (PLATE 34).[83] Two years after Othon de la Roche became duke of Athens in 1207, he gave it to the Cistercian monks of the abbey of Bellevaux.[84] We have very scant information on the Latin period of Daphni. There are no archives left nor any pilgrims' descrip-

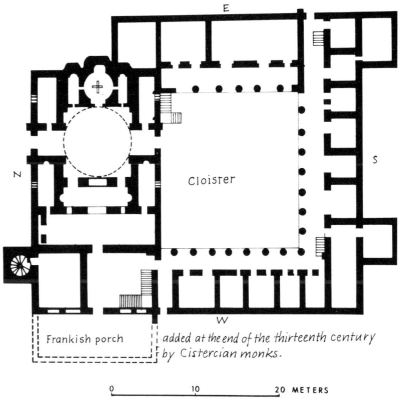

Fig. 9. *Plan of the church of Daphni.*

tions.[85] The church of Daphni was known under the French name of Dalphin or Dalphiner, derived from the Greek name Daphnion, Daphnin, or Daphni, given because of the many laurels in the region.[86] Although Cistercian monks generally did not use monasteries built by other monks, they nevertheless stayed in Daphni two and a half centuries, until 1458, and retained the buildings almost as they took them over. At the time of the architectural restorations made by Stikas in 1959, it was determined that no alterations had been made to the church itself or to the other buildings of the abbey, and that even the porch of the church, which has Latin features, was not a Cistercian addition.[87] The cloister to the south of the church, which Buchon, Lenormant, and Millet had taken for a Cistercian construction, is, according to Orlandos,[88] of a much more recent period. The entrance on the eastern side of

Plate 34. Monastery of Daphni. Western facade after the restoration (1969).

the abbey, surmounted by a pointed arch, is of the same more recent period as the cloister. The construction probably belonged to the sixteenth century and, in spite of the pointed arches, were the work of the Greek monks who returned to the abbey after the departure of the Cistercians.[89] The best proof for this is the much less carefully executed building technique.

The Cistercian monks had established themselves in Daphni in 1211,[90] but it was only later, at the end of the thirteenth century or the beginning of the fourteenth, that the porch of the church was repaired.[91] Earthquakes had demolished the upper story and the facade of the Byzantine outer narthex (PLATE 35).

Plate 35. Monastery of Daphni. Western facade beginning of the fourteenth century.

THE WESTERN PART OF THE CHURCH

The exterior. The Byzantine exonarthex was built later than the rest of the church and leaned only against the western wall of the narthex (PLATE 36).[92] The basic structure of this porch dates from the twelfth century, the same period as the upper story, of which almost nothing remains. A square tower with a winding staircase, placed against the northern wall of the porch and leading to the upper story, is also from the twelfth century. This portal was not an integral part of the church, and the weight of the upper story probably brought about the destruction of the portal's western wall and its roof.

Because of this the Cistercian monks were forced to rebuild the western facade (PLATE 37). They replaced the two earlier round arches with two pointed arches supported by two rectangular pillars on each side of the facade. In the center they placed a wider pointed arch. On the left side, however, they retained a small Byzantine arch, apparently to balance the entrance.[93] This portal extended along the facade of the church and must have resembled

Plate 36. Daphni. Porch, exterior view of southern side, view fom the cloister (twelfth century).

the one in the church of the Cistercian abbey of Pontigny;[94] large porches across the width of the church were very common in Burgundy.[95] The arcade of Pontigny, however, is very shallow, placed against a wall and held up by small coupled colonnettes placed on very tall bases, giving the appearance of balanced classical proportions. The arcade of Daphni, quite differently constructed, looks more severe and is much higher. It was restored in the 1960s by Stikas.[96]

Plate 37. Daphni. Porch, interior view of north-west corner (twelfth-century Byzantine work and the fourteenth-century Cistercian addition).

The pointed arches are placed very high on simple rectangular pillars without engaged colonnettes. The imposts on which the arches rest have shallow parallel fluting with a decoration of barley stalks such as can be seen on many Cistercian pillars.[97] No tracery seems to have been done on these arches, for nothing was found during the restoration.[98] The pointed arches were decorated by a simple fillet that stops on the imposts. Before the reconstruction of the portal, it was not possible to see that there was an arcade rather than a portal between two-light windows; we have several descriptions of this.[99]

The arcade of Daphni's portal must be dated later than Zaraka's windows. The general shape of the arcade recalls the arcade of the apse of the cathedral of Narbonne, constructed at the end of the thirteenth century, and the nave of Palma de Mallorca, constructed at the beginning of the fourteenth century. These have very simple pillars with capitals placed very high, making the pillars look tall and attenuated.[100] It is difficult to know how this Gothic style of southern France was transplanted into Greece at the end of the thirteenth century or the beginning of the fourteenth —just at a time when all Cistercian abbeys of continental Greece had been abandoned. The General Cistercian Chapter states in 1276 that Daphni alone survives. But even in 1306 the situation still appeared satisfactory enough for Daphni, for at the request of the bishop of Cephalonia and of Princess Isabella of Achaia, the pope, Clement V, put under its protection and guidance the church of Santa Maria de Camina of the diocese of Olenos.[101]

One must of course remember that Cistercian diffusion in the thirteenth and fourteenth centuries was not restricted by political limitations. But the French remained the masters of the duchy of Athens until the end of the first decade of the fourteenth century, and after this the duchy fell into the hands of the Catalans (1311–87), who probably encouraged the importation of their compatriot monks. When the Catalans settled in Attica, they undertook to reorganize the land as well as the church.[102] They placed Spaniards at the head of the bishoprics, and the bishops were appointed by the king of Sicily.[103]

No document has survived that speaks of this period of Daphni. We know only the names of certain abbots, such as Peter in 1283, James in 1308, John Fondremand in the fourteenth century, and Peter Strosberch in 1412.[104] Although our information remains scanty, we can at least judge stylistically that the facade of Daphni dates from the thirteenth century or at the latest from the first part of the fourteenth century, rather than immediately after the arrival of the Cistercians. On the southwestern side of the church wall, two circular Byzantine arches are left, built of two rows of brick supported by an ancient column with an Ionic capital. The western facade had similar arches before the Cistercian reconstruction. The northern side has an arcade that ends against a square tower.

The interior side of the portal. The portal is covered by groin vaults in a manner conforming with other parts of the eleventh-century church. The area originally supporting the groin vaults is clearly visible in the southwestern angle.[105] The porch was divided into three bays, and the vaults were supported by antique columns on the side of the narthex. These columns were shipped to England by Lord Elgin in the last century. Over the portal, the Cistercian monks did not rebuild the second floor. They only placed crenelations all along the three walls, giving the church a more forbidding, fortified look. One can find a resemblance between the upper part of this wall and the facade of Saint Denis, which antedates it by a century. The monks of Daphni needed protection from pirates who could attack them from the bay of Saronikos, and they even added an *assommoir* on the southern side, which existed until 1877. It is visible on a watercolor by M. Benouville, over the southern false arcade.[106]

The Cistercians also changed the barrel-vaulted crypt of the church narthex, transforming it into a funerary chapel for the Frankish dukes of Athens. By receiving with fervor the remains of their benefactors, they encouraged generosity toward their monastic order.[107] The general chapter gave the Cistercian monasteries permission for burial in 1217. A document in 1308 of Father James, abbot of Daphni, relates that Guy II (de la Roche), who died on 6 October 1308, was buried with his ancestors in the abbey of Daphni.[108] The crypt was accessible from the northern side of the narthex and did not continue under the church proper. The Catalans who governed the duchy of Athens from 1311 to 1387, in contrast to the Frankish dukes, preferred to be buried in the Latin church of the Virgin of the Parthenon on the Acropolis, as was the Italian Nerio Acciajuoli in 1394.[109] In 1276 the monastery of Daphni was the only Cistercian foundation on the Greek peninsula.[110] The Cistercians left Daphni only after the arrival of Mohammed II in Athens in 1458.

The Monastery of Gergeri on the Island of Crete

Gergeri, in the province of Candia, had been a Greek monastery before 1210, when the patriarch of Constantinople, under Venetian influence, requested that the general chapter place the monastery of Mount Sancti Gregori under the jurisdiction of the Cistercian monastery of Saint Thomas of Torcello. It is known that the request was granted, but there is no information on the monastery itself, which has disappeared. We also know that the monks of Saint Thomas occupied the monastery on 30 May 1218, replacing the Greek monks, and that on 22 November 1223 Honorius III wrote to the archbishop of Crete to ask him to help the monks of Saint Thomas. These monks cultivated the land that had been given to them in Crete and were demanding a place where they could "rest their heads."[111] Gergeri continued as a Cistercian monastery for several centuries, even after the other Cistercians of Greece had returned to the West.

Saint Mary Varangorum of Crete

The Cistercian monastery of Saint Mary Varangorum had been offered in June 1230 by Giacomo Tiepolo, doge of Venice, to Saint Thomas of Torcello. Today there is nothing left of it; it is known to us only by name, and we can not even pinpoint its location. In 1273, fifty-five years after the Cistercian monks were established at Gergeri, the abbey of Saint Thomas asked permission from the general chapter to send monks to Crete[112] and establish the monastery of Saint Mary Varangorum. In 1340, however, this monastery seems to have been abandoned by the Cistercian monks.

4 *The Churches of the Mendicant Orders in Greece*

The Architecture of the Preaching Friars and Minorites

The preaching friars and minorites spread out into the Latin Empire of Constantinople starting in 1220, soon after the founding of their orders.[1] Both orders had placed themselves in the service of the pope and of the Latin patriarchate to consolidate the ecclesiastical union and to try to stabilize the church of Constantinople economically and politically. They established themselves in the capital and in the most important centers. The sources that refer to them are scanty, and several of their buildings have been destroyed. Others still exist but are in shambles. Regardless of all this, the documents and constructions that are preserved shed enough light to let one evaluate the Western influence of the mendicant orders on Greece after the Fourth Crusade. The preaching friars are also known as Dominican fathers, for the founder of the order, Saint Dominic. The origin of the order is tied to the crusade against the Albigenses. In 1204, after a mission to Denmark, Saint Dominic was persuaded by Pope Innocent III to help the Cistercians, to whom he had assigned the task of combating the Albigensian heresy in the Languedoc.[2] It was in the south of France, in the vicinity of Toulouse, that the Dominican order took shape.

The Dominican buildings, like the Cistercian ones, were strikingly simple. Saint Dominic wanted poverty to be apparent and thought the monasteries of the preaching fathers should be characterized by modesty and humility. Neither Dominican nor Cistercian architecture was regulated by a legislature or by positive rules on how to build; they followed restrictive prescriptions:[3] the height of the walls of the monastic buildings could not surpass 4.50m for the ground floor or 7.50m for the second floor. The height of the church was set at 11.40m, and its ceiling could not be vaulted in stone except over the choir and the apse.[4] The rule against vaults over the nave and aisles was also mentioned after 1260 in the Franciscan statutes, which even forbade vaults over the choir except over the apse itself.[5]

Although these rules were probably followed at the beginning, later—as in the Cistercian churches—they were often ignored. Unfortunately, even in the West we have no extant example of Dominican architecture from before 1240, and we are dependent on details mentioned in chronicles. It is thus impossible to know exactly to what extent the rules were followed until this period.

The primary vocation and dedication of the Dominicans was to preach as often as possible away from their monasteries; so their churches did not need to be spacious. Their sermons were directed to crowds who did not go to church or to the faithful who met in parochial churches. The Dominicans lived communally in monastic buildings adjacent to the church, the cloister and the church forming a unit exactly like those in the Cistercian monasteries, which they frequently imitated. Often, however, the Dominican fathers preferred to establish themselves in the towns or in the densely populated neighborhoods outside the towns themselves. Because of this they were forced to keep their buildings closer together, for the land given to them was less extensive, and they had to consider the neighboring buildings, the streets, and the availability of water. Their buildings were often more restricted than those of the Cistercians or the Premonstratensians, who settled in the country.[6] The mendicant orders had to accommodate themselves to circumstances and, too often, had to accept existing churches. Their architecture has a family air that one can recognize in spite of its variety of forms.

The Dominicans willingly followed the architectural habits and customs of the Cistercians, if these were compatible with their own apostolic mission, and accepted almost no decoration in their churches. They had no fixed resources like the chapters, the abbeys, and the parochial churches and were forced to limit their expenses, unless they happened to find a benefactor, which seldom occurred. As a result, the buildings of the Dominicans stand out for their architectural monumentality owing to their insistence on simplicity and austerity, which often surpasses even that of the Cistercian churches.

Saint Sophia of Andravida, a Dominican Church

Andravida,[7] the capital of the kingdom of Achaia, had become under Geoffrey I (1210–1228/30) the episcopal seat of the bishop of Olena. According to the Aragonian chronicle, William II of Villehardouin (1246–78) had built there the churches of Saint Sophia, Saint Stephen, and Saint James: "Et ordano en reuerencia de Dios et fiso fer en Andreuilla tres eglesias es a saber: la yglesia de Santa Sofia de los Frayres Predicatores, et Sant Steuan de los Frayres Menores et Sant Jayme de los Templeros que aguora es de los Espitaleros."[8] In reality the church of Saint James had existed since before 1214, and Geoffrey I and his family were buried there. The Templars acquired it in 1241.[9] Of the church of Saint Stephen nothing is known, though we have good reason to believe it was the Franciscan church mentioned in the annals of the order.[10] As for Saint Sophia, it is quite plausible that it was built during the reign of William II. It was a Dominican church, large enough, according to the chronicle, to be used as an assembly place more than once during William's reign.[11] We know almost nothing about its construction, and only some of the architectural details may give us some clue about its date.[12] From the sources one can deduce that it could not have been built by the Dominicans before 1240 because they established themselves in the Latin Empire after this date.[13]

DESCRIPTION OF THE CHURCH

The only visible ruins are those of the church of Saint Sophia itself; there are no traces of the abbey. The church was a long basilica with three naves and no apparent transept having a square apse and two rectangular chapels at the end of each aisle. The sanctuary and the two chapels to the east are better preserved than the rest of the church (PLATE 38). The length of this part of the building is approximately 4.60m and the width 18.90m (FIG. 10).

The nave was twice as wide as the aisles. One can still see the foundations of the bases of several columns that must have carried the arcades dividing the aisles from the nave (PLATE 39). Only one base remains, and it has a simple torus on a plinth. According to Rennell Rodd, there were originally ten columns of granite, four of which were transported to the neighboring village of Lechania and reused in another church.[14] But there is no proof of this hypothesis, and none of the columns was found in place.[15] The nave and the aisles must have been covered by a pointed wooden roof.

THE SANCTUARY

The choir of Saint Sophia forms a rectangle with two bays covered

Plate 38. Saint Sophia of Andravida. Dominican church. Second quarter of the thirteenth century. View from the east of the sanctuary and south chapel.

Plate 39. Saint Sophia of Andravida. Choir and chapels, western view.

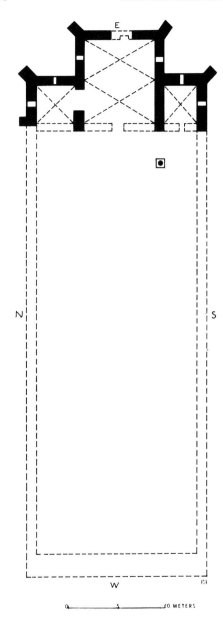

by ribbed vaults, without a tranverse arch. It is flanked on both sides by rectangular chapels, also vaulted by quadripartite ribbed vaults. The chapels and the choir are divided by walls without openings. Later a door was opened between the choir and the northern chapel. The apse extends 4.60 m farther out from the chapels (FIG. 10). It is lit by three windows: two are very tall and narrow, crowned with round arches. The third, which dominates the eastern side (PLATE 40), is much larger and has a pointed arch.

Fig. 10. The Dominican church of Saint Sophia of Andravida. Middle of the thirteenth century. Plan of the church.

Plate 40. Saint Sophia of Andravida. Choir, interior view.

The interior of the northern chapel measures 3.65 m × 3.50 m. It has two windows, on the north and on the east; both have rounded arches but are not as tall as those of the apse. The southern chapel has the same proportions and the same windows as the northern chapel, but its ribbed vault is placed higher, indicating that the two chapels were not built simultaneously. There is a strange difference in the widths of the openings of the two chapel arcades and that of the choir onto the nave and aisles. The central opening is 6.65 m, the northern 3.50 m, and the southern much smaller, 2.82 m. The southern chapel, which also has a higher vault, seems not to have been included in the original plan of the church but was probably added later. The floor of the choir is approximately 1 m higher than the floor of the nave and must have been reached by a few stairs. The chapels were lower; today their floors are raised by an accumulation of debris, but in the Frankish period they must have been at the same level as the aisles.[16] The arches that separate the aisles and nave from the chapels are pointed, with projecting voussoirs that abut on engaged columns. The arcade of the southern chapel is narrower and is placed lower than the corresponding northern one. This lack of uniformity between the two chapels is puzzling; though the southern chapel was probably added later, we have no proof of it.

The masonry of the aisle is made of blocks of limestone intermingled with blocks of porous stone, some of which came from antique buildings in the vicinity. They are carefully worked. One can still see the imposts that supported the arcade separating the nave from the two side aisles. There seem to have been no pilasters or engaged columns under these. A modern wall was built across the central bay of the choir, but it has been partially removed by the archeological service of Anastylosis. The entrance to the northern chapel is, however, still blocked by such a wall.

The Exterior of the Building

Of the northern, southern, and western facades practically nothing is left of the superstructure. The walls measured approximately 0.90 m in thickness, except on the western facade, where the thickness was almost doubled to approximately 2 m. Traquair suggested that perhaps the facade had a certain importance. According to Bon, there must have been several portals preceded by porches.[17]

The exterior walls of the eastern side are built in ashlar like the one that faces the nave and aisles. In certain spots pieces of brick were used to fill small openings among the stones, a practice popular in Byzantine architecture.

Buttresses placed diagonally reinforce the angles of the chapels and the apse (PLATE 41). Similar buttresses probably existed against the northern and southern walls. One still remains, perpendicular to the wall at the northwest angle of the northern chapel. At this corner one can still see traces of a staircase that belonged to a Turkish minaret. During the Turkish occupation, the large eastern window was shortened and a mihrab was added (PLATE 42). This part of the church was used as a mosque at the time.

Plate 41. *Saint Sophia of Andravida. Buttresses of the sanctuary and southern chapel.*

Plate 42. *Saint Sophia of Andravida. Choir window.*

The roofs of the chapels and the choir are more recent than the church, but they probably differed little from the earlier ones except that they may have been more steeply inclined.

The church of Saint Sophia must have been very large and probably had ten bays. It also seems to have possessed a transept not extending over the width of the main church.[18] The roof of the nave was probably slightly higher than that of the aisles, if one is to judge from the difference between the height of the apse and the chapels.

DECORATIVE DETAILS

The ribs of the vaults have the form of a torus placed on a flat band, which creates a certain heavy appearance (PLATE 43). Those of the northern chapel start very low on the wall and fall back on capitals decorated by naturalistically carved leaves.[19] The capitals rest on columns less than 1 m in height (PLATE 44). The supports of the southern chapel are not very different but are more disfigured. Here the vaults are placed slightly higher and so is the window.[20] Under this window on the southern wall is a niche 1.80 m in height, 1 m in width, and 0.50 m in depth, crowned by a trefoil framed by rounded molding (PLATE 45).

Plate 43. Saint Sophia of Andravida. Ribs of the choir vault.

Plate 44. Saint Sophia of Andravida. Northern chapel. Capital of the northeastern corner.

Plate 45. Saint Sophia of Andravida. Niche in the southern chapel.

The ribs of the choir are gathered together on an octagonal tas-decharge that rests on the capitals of the small columns, only slightly taller than those of the chapels. Keystones in the form of simple roses or other motifs are still in place at the crossing of the ribs (PLATE 52). The small columns are placed only at the corners of the choir and are crowned by capitals on which the ribs rest. The other ribs rest on corbels placed in the center of the south and north walls. The corbel on the south wall is decorated by a head, which unfortunately is greatly mutilated (PLATE 46).

Plate 46. Saint Sophia of Andravida. Detail of choir; corbel on south side with human head.

Plate 48. Saint Sophia of Andravida. Choir capital in the southeastern corner.

The capitals in the corners have groups of two and three small rounded leaves on long stalks (PLATE 48). Among them there are simple flat leaves. The capitals of the two engaged columns that support the triumphal arch of the choir have the same motifs as the angle capitals of the choir (PLATES 48, 49, 51). They can be compared with the capitals of the Cistercian church of Epau at Sarthe and of the Cour Dieu of Loiret, built in 1170 and 1216.[21] This type of leaf that ends in a slightly pointed ball or a bud is another version of leaves forming hooks that are very common in Cistercian churches of the twelfth century but that can still be found even into the thirteenth century.[22] The head decorating the corbel in the choir is also often found in the West in the thirteenth century. The one at Saint Sophia has been compared with one found at Villelongue, Aude, from the second half of the thirteenth century. But one can also mention the head of a devil on a corbel of the Cistercian monastery of Senanque in France, which dates from the end of the twelfth century (PLATE 47). It is difficult to know exactly what the head in the church in Andravida represents, for it is too mutilated.

Plate 47. Senanque. Devil's head forming a corbel.

Plate 49. Saint Sophia of Andravida. Southwest capital supporting the central arch of the choir.

Plate 51. Saint Sophia of Andravida. Capital at the northwestern side of the choir.

Around the sanctuary, at 1.25 m above the ground, a thick band runs over the little columns like a ring and crowns another niche in the wall under the eastern window (PLATE 50). This window (1.40 m in width), in the choir, is the one that was shortened by the Turks. By its size, it dominates this part of the church. Its pointed arch is simply rounded off, but the opening itself is surrounded by a projecting molding applied against the jambs. Nothing has been found of the tracery of this window. It must have been divided in two by a small column that corresponds to the jambs on both sides of the window. It is impossible to imagine what the tracery was like, since not even the exact date of construction of the church is known. It could be like that at Zaraka or like that of Our Lady of Isova,[23] or it could have had three trefoils forming a triangle, which would have given it a lacier appearance. There was no glass in any of the windows, but they were protected by iron bars whose holes can still be seen in the wall. In the southern wall there are certain indications that another building leaned against the southern chapel. There is no information about its date or its purpose, and no vestiges were found of monastery buildings.

Plate 50. Saint Sophia of Andravida. Niche in the choir.

Plate 52. Saint Sophia of Andravida. Southern chapel, keystone.

The church of Saint Sophia at Andravida is purely Western. One can say with conviction that it has a great deal in common with other Dominican churches of the West, according with the general characteristics already enumerated. Meerseman divided Dominican architecture into three periods. The first is the period of conception (1216–40); the second of infancy (from 1240); and the third of adolescence (1264–1300).[24] Saint Sophia seems to belong to the second period, when the Dominicans preferred a deeper and larger apse and accepted a few decorative motifs. They retained, however, the ascetic and practical spirit of the first years of the order. Saint Sophia cannot be considered as depending on a particular school of France but rather shows a preference for the most economical and simple forms.[25] The financial means of the Dominican fathers were meager. Wherever they had to build their own churches, they depended on donations. At Andravida they must have obtained the help of princes, since Saint Sophia played the role of a cathedral; but even in this case they had to remain faithful to their principles of humility.

Plate 53. Capital with coat of arms deposited at Saint Sophia.

Plate 54. Other side of capital shown in plate 53.

The adopted forms are simple and remind one strongly of those of the Cistercians. The single-light windows, which must have continued on the exterior of the aisle, already existed in Romanesque buildings but continue to appear a century later in the Gothic style of monastic buildings of several Western countries.[26] There is most of all a common appearance between the monastic churches of Greece built during the thirteenth century by Westerners. Our Lady of Zaraka, Our Lady of Isova, and Saint Sophia of Andravida resemble each other not only in their general plans but even in their details. One can speak not of a traveling workshop that worked in all three of these churches, but rather of a common spirit in the monks' building.[27]

There are many archaic details at Saint Sophia just like those in the other churches. The ribs of the rib vault and the sculptural decor of many of the capitals are more closely related to the twelfth century than to the thirteenth, but the window of the eastern wall of the choir of Saint Sophia must date from near the middle of the thirteenth century. The buttresses at the angles also indicate that the monks did not ignore the more advanced methods practiced in the West. However, the decoration of the capitals of the northern chapel in particular, though simple, shows the naturalistic interest of artists in the thirteenth century (PLATES 47 and 48). It seems much too late to place Saint Sophia at the beginning of the fourteenth century as Traquair does,[28] for none of the characteristics mentioned is necessarily from that period. A capital with a coat of arms of Achaia and of Hainaut that is now in the apse of Saint Sophia does not belong to this church (PLATES 53 and 54). According to Sotiriou, it belongs to the church of Saint Stephen's, where it was found 3 m deep in the ground.[29] It is, then, quite probable that Saint Sophia was constructed under William II of Villehardouin, as was stated in the chronicle—but in the first years of his reign.

The Franciscan Church of the Monastery of Vlachernes

The monastery of Vlachernes, not far from Andravida and Clarence in a very fertile part of Morea, was occupied in the thirteenth century by Latin monks, probably Franciscans.[30] Even though no historical document on this subject has been found, nor any mention of its existence in the chronicle, the church of this monastery has been the object of several archeological and architectural studies (PLATE 56).

Orlandos, who studied it in 1923, considers the main part of the church Byzantine of the twelfth century. At the beginning of the

Plate 55. Tombstone of Princess Agnes (1286) deposited at Saint Sophia.

thirteenth century, it was probably occupied by Franciscan monks. Bon believes the church was not completely finished when the Franks established themselves in Morea in 1205 and thinks they were the ones who made the addition we have today.[31]

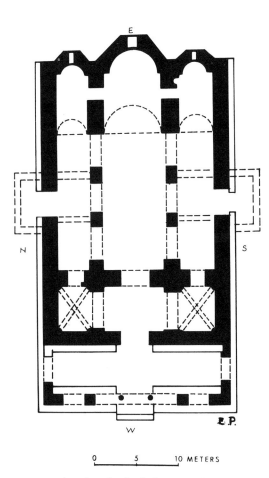

Fig. 11. The church of Vlachernes. The additions made by the Franciscan monks date from the beginning of the thirteenth century.

Plate 56. Church of Vlachernes. Western facade. Early thirteenth century.

Since this is a Byzantine building, we need mention only that the plan of the church is that of a basilica with a nave and two aisles divided into three bays each. Its eastern end is formed by three rounded apses on the inside and half a hexagon on the outside, as is usual in Byzantine sanctuaries. On the west side one enters the church through a porch leading to a narthex of three bays (FIG. 11).

The upper part of the porch has a room now divided by modern walls into five small compartments (PLATE 57). Inside this room is a two-light window opening toward the nave and the aisles that, before this upper room was added by the Frankish monks, must have been part of the western facade of the Byzantine church. According to inscriptions, the porch and the facade as they are today were reconstructed by Greek monks during the eighteenth century.[32] According to Orlandos, the Latin monks retained the monastery of Vlachernes even after the Turkish occupation, until the seventeenth century.

The interest of this church lies particularly in the details that were added during renovations by the Latin monks, and in the successful way these decorations were integrated with the Byzantine architecture. It is one of the very rare examples in Greece where Western medieval art appears so well blended with Byzantine elements, forming a new type of architecture.

Plate 57. Church of Vlachernes. Southern view.

Plate 58. Church of Vlachernes. Southern side.

THE EXTERIOR OF THE CHURCH

The eastern wall and the walls of the side aisles, the ground story of the narthex, and the upper part of the nave are built of ashlar placed very regularly and separated by bricks. The upper story of the narthex, all of the western side, as well as the gable and the angles of the sanctuary to the east are built of blocks of porous stone without bricks (PLATE 58).

This difference lets one conjecture that there were two building stages in the construction besides the one of the western facade, whose date we know from the inscription. Although we know that the second stage is reminiscent of a Western approach to buildings, without bricks intermingled with the ashlar, one cannot be positive that at Vlachernes this part of the church belongs to the Frankish construction of the thirteenth century. This type of building method had already appeared in Greece under Western influence in the twelfth century. Another example in support of this argument is furnished by the Byzantine church of Paleopanagia in Manolada, whose facade was completely executed in ashlar without brick, and which, according to Bouras, was built at the same time as the rest of the church and belongs to the period before the Crusaders arrived in Greece.[33]

Another even more interesting feature of the church of the Virgin of Vlachernes is the exterior cornice ornamented with rosettes at the top of the nave, which rests on thirteen consoles of porous stone (PLATE 58). Some are decorated with vertical bands; others, like the fourth one on the southeastern side, carry the head of an animal.[34] The seventh on the same side represents a lion resting on his left front paw, with his right front paw lifted in the air; he turns his head to the rear. This is a motif of Eastern provenance very often found in Greece but also well known in the West.[35]

At the corners of the walls of the nave and of the upper story of the narthex rise little columns ending in capitals (PLATE 59). These capitals are formed of simple blocks and are decorated with interlaced serpents or with a human face, as at Andravida. Small columns at the angles appear also at the windows of Andravida, as well as at Our Lady of Isova, and without doubt are of Western origin.

At Paleopanagia (Manolada) the northern and southern angles of the western facade of the church also have small columns, but without capitals or bases. This peculiarity, as well as the construction method of the walls, was the reason this part of the church of Vlachernes was attributed by Orlandos to the Frankish period. Though this opinion is not so widely held today, these details certainly indicate a Western influence that is rare in Greece and that appeared as early as the twelfth century. It is even more extraordinary to see these small columns appear at the end of the twelfth century in churches that are completely Byzantine, for example, at the angles of the windows of the main apse of the church of the Dormition of the Virgin at Merbeka in Argolis.[36]

The sources for these influences are not well known, but it is known that the Byzantine Empire, since the eleventh century and especially in the twelfth century under Emmanuel II Comnenos, had cultivated commercial relations with the Western Mediter-

Plate 59. Church of Vlachernes. Detail of the southern side.

Plate 60. *Church of Vlachernes. Detail of a southern window.*

Plate 61. *Church of Vlachernes. Detail of the northern door.*

ranean and especially Venice. The windows of the church of the Virgin of Vlachernes, which date from the twelfth century, are small and simple, with round arches. Those of the narthex were shortened and enlarged when another floor was added over the narthex.

On the first floor one can see two openings to the north as well as to the south (PLATE 60). On the north side, one of them is a very narrow door leading to a stone staircase (PLATE 61). It is flanked by two small columns whose capitals are sculptured and support a pointed arch with a molding not as wide as the columns. On top there is a brick chevron pattern that forms a second pointed arch and continues on the wall to the east and the west. It resembles in some ways the Norman Gothic friezes of chevrons that one also finds in Sicily. The entire doorway is ornamented by a stone archivault decorated with small cusped flowers, interrupted by a projection on each side of the pointed side of the arch. The second opening on the north side and on the same floor was framed in wood, in a more recent period, but seems to have originally had a pointed arch.

On the southern side the wall is pierced by two windows, the largest of them a double-light window. It is framed by the same thin columns and decorations as the door on the north side, but here a molding forming a torus draws a pointed arch that rests on the capitals of the columns. A small octagonal column of white marble surmounted by a Byzantine capital divides the two lights. The two ogival arches over these lights, made of porous stone, continue without interruption on the sides up to the window lintel. The tympanum is modern. The interior form of the window is certainly not purely Western and seems to be the work of a Greek mason. The second window is much smaller and has a round arch.

An earthquake in the eighteenth century necessitated the alterations to the western facade. It is possible that other repairs were also made on the north side, where the cornice and the chevron brick decoration that ornament the southern pediment over the large window and all the other parts of the church are missing.

THE INTERIOR OF THE CHURCH

The narthex is divided in three parts that correspond to the nave and the aisles of the naos. The central part is covered by a small low dome, while the almost square bays on the north and south are covered by ribbed vaults. In each corner small colonnettes of gray marble rise, placed on bases. Their capitals are decorated with flat

leaves, of a rather archaic style and with volutes (PLATE 62).[37] One can distinguish four types of capitals. The ribs are in the form of simple toruses 0.10 m thick. The keystones represent a lamb on the north side and a dove on the south (PLATE 63).

The construction of these ribs made it necessary to transform the window on the south side. The narthex is the only side of the church covered with ribbed vaults. On the nave a ceiling hides a peaked wooden roof, while the side aisles have long running barrel vaults slightly wider than a quarter circle. This form of vault was known since early in Romanesque architecture; it was used over side aisles and often on galleries (PLATE 64). In Byzantine architecture, where the usual form was the dome, groin vaults and barrel vaults were rarely placed at the angles of buildings, but this was done in many churches of the northeast Peloponnesus. Their dating remains uncertain, and the problem of their provenance is still hard to solve.[38] For this reason it is also difficult to know whether the running vaults of Vlachernes are a part of the project accomplished after the arrival of the Franks, at the same time as the vaults of the narthex and the cornice of the nave, or whether they were constructed during the twelfth century. None of the churches of purely Western style that have already been examined had such vaults.

Plate 62. Church of Vlachernes: (a-d) capitals of the narthex.

Plate 63. Church of Vlachernes. Southern ribbed vault and keystone of the narthex.

Plate 64. Church of Vlachernes. Vault of the southern aisle.

They can, however, be found at Saint Francis in Canea in the fourteenth century. It seems reasonable to believe that the rampant barrel vaults of Vlachernes, like the colonnettes at the angles and the stone masonry without brick, are Western forms, but that they may have been imported to Greece not after the arrival of the Crusaders, but earlier in the twelfth century. In Vlachernes we know that the wall without bricks and the colonnettes at the angles were built during the occupation of the Franciscan monks; but without clearing the wall of its plaster it is impossible to know whether the rampant vaults were also added in the thirteenth century.

According to Traquair, the church of the Virgin of Vlachernes shows three stages of construction. The first is Byzantine but influenced by the West; the second, which included the gallery over the narthex, is Angevin, influenced by southern Italy; and the third, which includes the porch and the west facade, is of the seventeenth and eighteenth centuries. Traquair places the construction of the room over the narthex in the fourteenth century, but before 1375.[39] According to Orlandos and Bon, the principal parts of the church are of the twelfth century, while the gallery over the narthex and the upper parts of the church were finished by the monks who settled there in the thirteenth century. If, as Orlandos says, these monks were Franciscans, the church can certainly not have been completed by them before 1220, for they established themselves in the Latin empire of Greece after 1219.[40]

There is absolutely no reason to accept Traquair's opinion that the second stage of the construction dates from the fourteenth century. Nothing in the Western forms of the ribbed vaults or in the decorations of the capitals indicates such a late date. On the contrary, the ribs and capitals, like the keystones, stand out because of their archaic character, which is here even more striking than in certain other Latin churches of the Peloponnesus already mentioned.

The Franciscan monks, like the Dominicans, were much more willing than the Cistercians to take over buildings built by other monks, even those built for a different rite. It is thus very possible that they established themselves in Vlachernes after the monastery was abandoned by the Greeks upon the arrival of the Latins. Perhaps the monastery had remained unoccupied for a time, since several lords had taken over the land and goods of the Orthodox clergy, and the church building had not been completed before the departure of the Greeks.

It is naturally difficult to accept the theory that the church was already complete and that the Latin monks demolished certain parts and built them up again. It is plausible that an earthquake or a fire could have destroyed the upper part of the church. The monks would in that case have hired Greek workers and shown them the Western formulas and construction methods they themselves were used to. The decorations around the openings of the northern and southern walls over the narthex remind one of southern Italy and Sicily. It is very likely that the Franciscan monks were Italian, since we know that Benedetto of Arezzo was one of the first Franciscans in Greece.

Traquair suggests a relationship between the Western details of Vlachernes and those of the Latin churches of Cyprus, which are, however, of a much later date.[41] The interest of the church of Vlachernes lies in the fusion of Western and Byzantine elements into a homogeneous whole. Certain of these forms had already been introduced before the thirteenth century; it will be interesting to see whether they were perpetuated in other buildings across Greece.

The Churches of the Mendicant Orders in Candia, Crete

As early as 1210 the Venetians had established in Crete a political, social and religious system on the plan of the *Serenissima* on the Adriatic (FIG. 12). Therefore, after the war against the Genoese Candia became the capital of the island and its most active center. It is here, on the "Piazza della Biada," that the duke's residence, the "Palazzo Ducale," and the "Palazzo del Capitan Generale" were situated. On the "Piazza dei Signori" were the "Palazzo del Capitan Grande" and the "Loggia." A third square was that of Saint Mark, which, like the one in Venice, was embellished with a church of Saint Mark.

Venice soon realized that its greatest problem in this newly occupied territory would be to impose the Roman Catholic rite on the population.[42] For this reason, besides patronizing the regular clergy, she also encouraged the establishment of monastic orders. Since the beginning of the thirteenth century these orders had acquired great influence across Europe. Franciscans, Dominicans, and Augustinians established themselves in almost every part of the island, especially in the larger cities of its Western section (FIG. 13).

Unfortunately, most of the churches here have suffered a great deal and are even harder to study than those on the mainland of Greece.[43] Since the most ancient times, Crete has periodically been

Fig. 12. Emblem of Venice. Drawing by Boschini, 1651.

PAX TIBI MAR CE EVAN GELIS TA MEVS

shaken by destructive earthquakes. During the Venetian occupation Candia (Herakleion) experienced four major earthquakes that repeatedly destroyed its Venetian churches.[44] Most of these were rebuilt, but they suffered again from the Turkish war of 1645–69. Since they were situated in the towns or in more populated centers where the Catholic church could reach more people, they were transformed after the departure of the Venetians: the Turks made them into mosques and in the twentieth century they were used as public buildings. Several were even destroyed by the local population, which had no appreciation for them. Since the beginning of this century, when Gerola visited a great number of these churches, many have disappeared completely and others have continued to deteriorate.

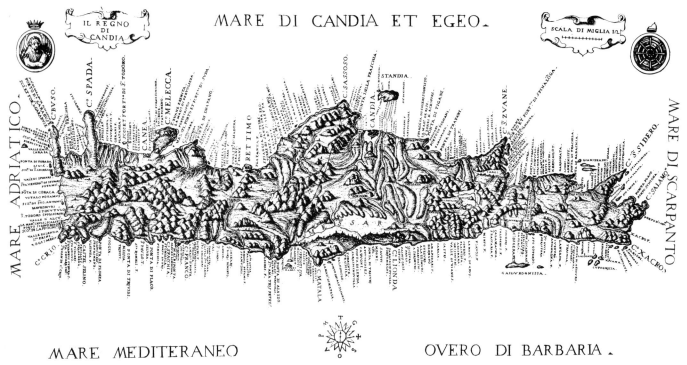

Fig. 13. Map of Crete. Drawing of the seventeenth century by Boschini.

Here we are dealing only with the ones that retain enough of the original construction to make study possible.[45] These churches are situated in the large centers of the island like Candia and Canea and have the same characteristically austere, logical, and simple plans as the mainland churches. Their sanctuaries, covered with ribbed vaults, are always square, and their elevation remains two-storied.

The influences on Crete, however, come from Italy rather than France, and the stylistic similarities are due not to the contact of Crete with mainland Greece, but to the traditions of the monastic orders.

Saint Peter Martyr

The church of Saint Peter is very close to the port of Candia and to the fortifications (FIG. 14). Such a location was common to the mendicant orders, who often formed new concentrations on the outskirts, away from the cathedral centers. The exact date of construction of this church is not known. The only available information is that it was built by Dominican fathers during the first half of the thirteenth century.[46] Large sections of the building were destroyed by earthquakes in 1303 and again in 1508. The Turks later rebuilt it, turning the church of Saint Peter into the mosque of Sultan Ibrahim.[47] Today it stands ruined and roofless, but showing clearer indications of the several alterations it suffered than some of the other churches of the island, which were restored and often whitewashed in recent years for use by the local community (PLATE 65).[48]

Plate 65. Saint Peter Martyr. Western facade.

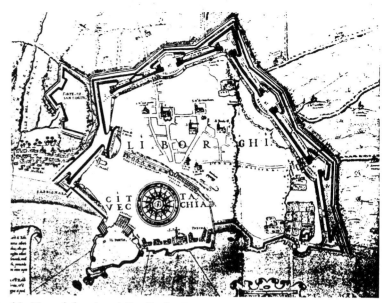

Fig. 14. Map of the city of Candia, by Rossi, 1573.

The plan. From the existing church and the plan of Gerola it seems that Saint Peter had a single nave approximately 41 m in length and 15 m in width. The square sanctuary has two bays and extends another 14 m beyond the nave (FIG. 16). Its interior dimensions are 6.50 m × 13 m. The walls have a thickness of approximately 1 m except on the western facade and part of the northern side of a small chamber that abuts on the choir, where they are slightly thicker. Two buttresses support the angles of the choir and project half a meter toward the east. During a second building stage, probably in the fourteenth century, two chapels were added on each side of the sanctuary. Both had the same length as the two bays of the choir and apse but extended over the width of the nave. The chapel to the north was already completely ruined in Gerola's time; in its place is the tiny vaulted room mentioned above. It is obvious that the church of Saint Peter had several stages of construction, but they are difficult to classify with certainty because of the lack of written information and the poverty of sculptural detail. A tall circular arch frames the choir and divides it from the nave, resting on two square pillars devoid of capitals and finished off by a very narrow plinth.[49] On both sides of this arch one can still see four arched openings that were later filled in with rubble. The two on top seem to have been windows with slightly pointed arches. The two below could have been niches used as entrances when the chapels were added. Seen from the west, this eastern wall must have resembled the eastern wall of the Franciscan church of Santa Croce in Florence.

The level of the ground inside the church is raised compared with the exterior, and so it is very probable that the arched entrances to the chapels were taller than they look today.

An indication of a third change made after the original construction, probably after the earthquake of 1508 or later, is the extension of the north and south walls of the nave, which abut onto the arcade between nave and sanctuary, blocking the arched openings just described (PLATE 66). Gerola's plan shows remnants of walls at right angles to the nave, both to the north and to the south of the church and extending as much as the chapels (FIG. 15). Thus it is natural to assume that the original plan of Saint Peter had a transept that was eliminated during the third building campaign (FIG. 16).

Plate 66. Saint Peter Martyr. The nave and choir.

Fig. 15. The church of Saint Peter Martyr, Candia. Plan by Gerola.

The north wall, completely reconstructed in the seventeenth century, has twelve windows, six in each of two rows, one above the other, which are of a later date than those of the southern wall (PLATE 67). Here too the walls must have been taller than they are today, for the windows on the first story are half hidden by the debris accumulated in the interior of the church. The building was used for services until recently, but restorations were started in 1974. The last window toward the east on the northern wall, the only circular window, is Turkish and has no counterpart in the other aisle windows. The west front now has an oculus where there seems to have originally been a large window. The small chamber at the north angle of the choir inside the northern chapel was used as a treasury. The inventories deposited there were transported to Venice at the time of the Turkish conquest.

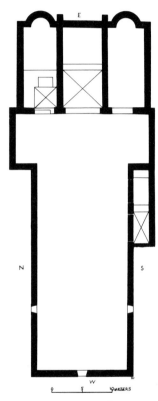

Fig. 16. *Saint Peter Martyr, Candia. Dominican church begun in the first half of the thirteenth century. Proposed plan.*

Plate 67. *Saint Peter Martyr. Northern wall (interior view)*

The exterior. On the southern side there are eight windows (PLATE 68), six of them crowned by circular arches. The first two on the west side had pointed arches and were filled in with rubble before the restoration. They are lancet windows, taller and thinner than the rest, and could be dated thirteenth century. Under the windows is an arcade of four pointed arches. The eastern two must have communicated with a small chapel of two bays, and the other two must have led originally to some of the other monastic buildings or to the cloister annexed to the main church. We know for certain, from a 1573 drawing by D. Rossi, that there was also a wall around the convent and a tower that was demolished by the Turks. Gerola mentions that one of the bays on the south side of the chapel was barrel-vaulted and the other was rib-vaulted.[50] Gerola's plan also shows traces of another small chapel to the south with a semicircular apse.[51] It is impossible to know when this chapel was added because it has completely disappeared. When the Turks transformed Saint Peter into a mosque, they added a minaret at the southwest corner, which was still standing when Gerola visited the church. On the west side a circular opening seems to have replaced an earlier large window whose traces can still be distinguished and which must once have dominated the facade (PLATE 65). All three sides of the church have entrances, but all of them seem to have been renovated and altered since the original church was built. The square east end, reinforced by two buttresses at the angles, also has a large round window (PLATE 69). One can still detect clear traces of two large windows with pointed arches that were later eliminated and replaced with the present round window.

Plate 68. Saint Peter Martyr. Southern wall (interior view)

Plate 69. Saint Peter Martyr. Eastern end.

The northern wall of the choir retains a large window with a pointed arch similar to the ones that existed on the east wall. Under this window the wall is plain, interrupted only by a very simple Gothic niche. The southwestern wall of the sanctuary, against

Plate 70. Saint Peter Martyr. The choir, interior view.

which the southern chapel was built, shows traces of enormous windows.

The first bay of the choir is covered by a domed ribbed vault (PLATE 70) reminiscent of the vaults of Lombardy, such as the one of Santa Maria del Carmine at Pavia. The ribs are rounded and heavy, and the vault itself is built of brick, also like Santa Maria del Carmine. The second bay of the sanctuary was rebuilt and now has a barrel vault (PLATES 71 and 72). In the corner one can still see half a shaft that carried the original ribbed vault. The southern chapel is covered by a barrel vault reinforced by two transverse arches (PLATE 73).[52] There is no direct communication between the choir and the chapels. On the eastern end is a large window, now blocked with rubble, that ends in a stilted arch.

Plate 71. Saint Peter Martyr. Choir vault; both bays and north wall.

Probably the northern chapel was vaulted in the same manner, while the treasury had a groin vault. Until the restoration the nave had a pointed wooden roof that rested on the sharp gable of the facade. The nave is slightly more elevated than the choir. The masonry of the church of Saint Peter does not show the careful craftsmanship of other Venetian buildings, except at the angles. The major part of the construction is done in stones of different dimensions, with no bricks. From several indications it seems probable that the church was whitewashed during the Turkish occupation. One can notice some painting under the wooden beams as in some of the other Venetian churches of Crete, but no traces of sculpural decorations are visible anywhere. The general forms and the details are characteristically simple.

Plate 72. Saint Peter Martyr. Choir vault.

The building is primarily impressive for its size and is also interesting for its general plan and many alterations. Its single nave, flat sanctuary, pointed wooden roof, and ribbed vaults are purely Western in style. Although there is a lack of the sculptural detail found in the Latin monastic churches of the Greek mainland, Saint Peter Martyr seems to belong to the same structural family group.

THE CHURCHES OF SAINT FRANCIS AND SAINT SALVADOR

Besides Saint Peter Martyr, the two most important monastic churches of Candia during the period of the Venetian domination were Saint Francis and Saint Salvador.

The monastery and church of Saint Francis have unfortunately disappeared. They were among the richest and most famous in Crete.[53] Built originally in 1242, the church was rebuilt at least twice, in the fourteenth century and in the sixteenth century, before being completely destroyed in 1856 by a second earthquake.[54] The Franciscan monks to whom it belonged lived there until the

Plate 73. Saint Peter Martyr. Southern chapel.

Plate 74. Saint Peter Martyr. Exterior southern wall of the choir and of the original transept.

Turkish occupation. On the site of the monastery today is the archeological museum of Herakleion.

The church of Saint Salvador existed until 1970. It had been converted into a high school for girls, but in 1970 it was demolished to make room for a parking lot. At the time Gerola visited it, it had been turned into a mosque by Sultan Validi. Before the Turkish occupation, this church belonged to Augustinian monks.

The plan of the church had one nave 44 m × 16 m that ended in a rectangular sanctuary (7 m × 9 m on the interior side). This sanctuary seems more modest and simple than the one of Saint Peter Martyr, and no modification altered its original form. Unfortunately, during the twentieth century the windows and facade were modernized and the building was turned into a high school, which of course altered its general appearance.

The wall of the nave was approximately 1 m thick, and nine buttresses reinforced the northern and southern sides and four the western facade. The buttresses at the western angles are more massive, and there are two more at the corners of the sanctuary on the eastern side. The windows that can be seen in the photos taken by Gerola are small and were placed rather high on the wall. They ended in pointed arches.

On the eastern side one could see traces of three lancet windows spread out over the whole surface of the wall between the buttresses. Gerola mentions that two of those windows were at one level and the third was higher up.[55] The church was covered by a pointed wooden roof resting on the very steep gable of the western facade. Gerola thought he saw the original roof, because some beams still showed traces of paint. But this seems very unlikely, since it is well known that this church, like the other churches of Candia, suffered from the 1508 earthquake. Only the rectangular choir, 11 m × 7.50 m, was covered by ribbed vaults whose three ribs were supported by corbels.

The western facade had three doors and a window below the gable. The church of Saint Salvador presented a more austere appearance than any of the other churches I have described. The exact date of its construction is unknown, but its plan was characteristic of the monastic buildings of the mendicant orders in Italy during the thirteenth century. Only descriptions of sixteenth- and seventeenth-century objects and paintings found within the church still exist. Several rich Venetians who had been patrons of this church were buried there. However, the demolition of 1970 destroyed even these last few remnants.

The Church of the Monastery of Saint Mary of the Crusaders (Crociferi)

The church of this monastery still exists in a very populated part of Candia. The monastery is mentioned for the first time in the acta of the fourteenth century, but the exact date of its construction is not known.[56] In 1501 the monastery was very poor and was left in the hands of a single chaplain. It was finally turned over to the Capuchins.[57] One must remember that the problems of the Latin clergy continued to worsen during the whole Venetian period. The monasteries and churches of Crete never enjoyed the same wealth as those in the West, even though some of them received rich family gifts from Venetians settled in Crete. The Venetian population was not large enough to maintain all the monastic churches of the island as well as those of the Latin clergy.[58] Furthermore, the Latin church of all Romania, as the Venetian states were otherwise known, was overshadowed by the Venetian political power abroad. The Venetians' expectations were such that they not only suppressed the local population but imposed on the Latin clergy the duty to help finance the community.[59] But the poverty of certain monasteries was not their sole concern. The hostility of the Greek population was breaking the enthusiasm of many monks, and the desertion of monastery and diocese became one of the gravest problems of the Catholic church.

The church of Saint Mary of the Crusaders in Candia was certainly not one of the richest or most important of the island or the town. But its plan, very similar to others already described, has a simple charm of its own. It is a basilica with a nave and two aisles 19 m in length. The central nave extends into a rectangular sanctuary that protrudes 4 m over the eastern exterior wall of the church (PLATE 75). The width of the central nave and of the choir is 5 m, and the side aisles are slightly narrower, 3.5 m (FIG. 17). The church is covered by an A-shaped tie-beam wooden roof over the central nave and the choir. The roof over the aisles is lower, thus allowing room for clerestory windows under the roof of the nave. A massive simplicity is communicated by the octagonal stone piers with Corinthian capitals that support the pointed arches dividing the nave and aisles (PLATE 76). A feeling of unity is ensured by the narrower side aisles and wide intercolumniation and by the definite horizontal accent throughout the building. The feeling and atmosphere are similar to the Franciscan church of San Lorenzo of Vicenza, built in 1281, which influenced Venetian architecture, even though there are many structural differences in the Cretan church.

Fig. 17. Saint Mary of the Crusaders (Crociferi). Fourteenth century. Plan of the church.

Plate 75. Saint Mary of the Crusaders (Crociferi) in Candia. The nave looking east.

Plate 76. Saint Mary of the Crusaders in Candia. Southern aisle.

The church was restored recently (PLATE 77). The piers were replaced, as well as the windows and doors, which are twentieth-century work. The church of Saint Mary served as a mosque under the Turks and was known as Anghebut Pascia o Chusciakli. The wall paintings that had existed before the Turkish occupation were destroyed by the Turks. There must have been monastic buildings and a cloister on the south side, and an arcade can still be seen in the southern wall (PLATE 78). These arches are reminiscent of the arches in the northern aisle wall of the Dominican church of the Jacobins in Toulouse.

Plate 77. *Saint Mary of the Crusaders in Candia. Exterior, south side.*

Plate 78. *Saint Mary of the Crusaders in Candia. Exterior view from the southwest.*

The Churches of the Mendicant Orders in Canea, Crete

The second town in Crete of great importance for Venice was Canea, in the western part of the island (FIG. 18). In some parts, Canea preserves better than Candia the atmosphere of the ancient Venetian city. A few efforts are slowly being made to free the Western buildings from Turkish and modern additions. Unfortunately, meticulous records are not being kept of the state of these buildings before and after the restoration, and they are often restored in such a manner that it is impossible to distinguish the additions or even the restored areas under the whitewash. Several buildings serve as storerooms, shops, housing, or even chicken coops and thus continue to deteriorate.

In the medieval period the most important monastic churches of the town were the Franciscan monasteries of Saint Francis and Saint Salvador, the Augustinian monastery of Saint Mary of Mercy, and the monastery of the Dominicans of Saint Nicolas (FIG. 19).[60] In 1539 the convent of Saint Mary had already suffered great destruction from the Turks. In 1583 a senate decree ordered the Venetian magistrates of Canea to help in the reconstuction of the convent. After the Turkish occupation, the church was again remodeled to serve as a mosque. Today only a few vestiges of the old Venetian church remain, among them part of the ribbed vault.

Fig. 18. The town of Canea. Map by Boschini, seventeenth century.

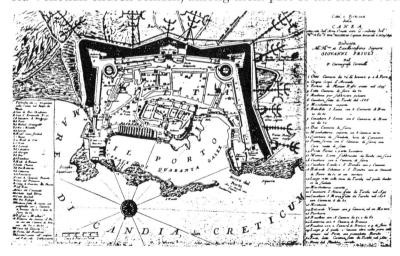

Fig. 19. The town of Canea. Map by Coronelli, 1689.

SAINT NICOLAS

The church of the monastery of Saint Nicolas now serves for the

Greek Orthodox rite, but one can recognize the general plan of
the Venetian monastery even after its modernization. The church
must date from the beginning of the fourteenth century: a decree
of 21 October 1320 mentions its construction by the Dominican
monks of Candia. During the Turkish period this church[61] was
converted into a mosque in the name of Sultan Ibrahim. The plan
of the church shows a basilica with a single nave 33m × 14m,
interrupted by a transept 19.40m in width. The choir, with its flat
eastern end, measures 11m in depth. This part is now separated
from the rest of the church by a modern inconostasis.

Two chapels with flat square apses are placed on either side of
the choir. The choir has two bays, the second half the width of the
first and extending 4m beyond the lateral chapels. On the northern
side of this bay was a bell tower that has now been completely
eliminated (FIG. 20).

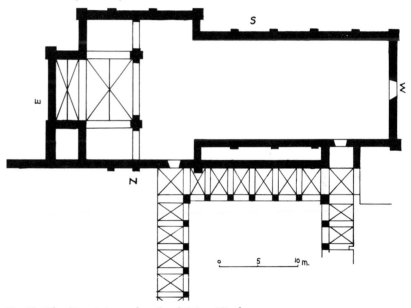

*Fig. 20. The Dominican church of Saint Nicolas
of Canea. About 1320.*

The masonry must have been of ashlar like that still to be seen
on the walls of the cloister (PLATE 79). The church is now covered
with plaster on both the outside and the inside. The windows and
doors have been replaced and do not belong to the medieval structure. In the interior, the choir and the two chapels are separated
from the single nave by an arcade of pointed diaphragm arches,

Plate 79. Saint Nicolas of Canea. The cloister.

Plate 80. Saint Nicolas of Canea. Ribbed vault of choir of the Dominican monastery built in the early fourteenth century.

accentuated by a single flat molding. The arch between the choir and the nave rests on square piers surrounded by four attached pilasters without capitals. The arcades of the chapels rest on the same pilasters and on simple pilasters attached to the north and south walls.

The two-bay choir is covered by ribbed vaults (PLATE 80). According to Gerola's plan, three ribs correspond to each bay, but in reality there are only two plus another that forms the transverse arch between the two bays.[62] This is a round arch and consequently is placed very low. The ribs have the form of a torus and rest on four small columns at the angles of the sanctuary (PLATE 81). Between the two bays, the ribs fall on corbels two-thirds of the way up the wall. The two chapels north and south of the choir are covered by barrel vaults (PLATE 82). Between the western bay of the choir and these chapels are openings covered by round arches with no sculptural decor.

Plate 81. Saint Nicolas of Canea. View of the sanctuary from the nave.

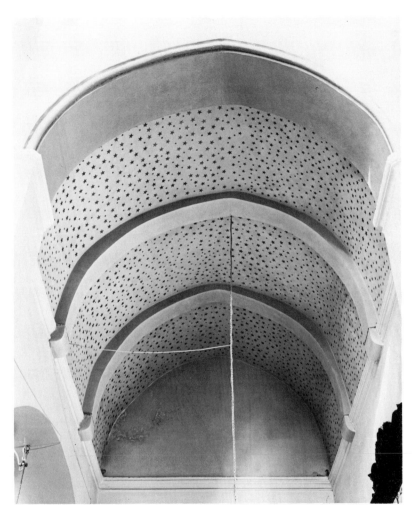

Plate 82. Saint Nicolas of Canea. Barrel vault of the southern chapel.

The nave of the church and the transept are covered by a flat ceiling that rests on the exterior walls of the building. The transept, which is larger than the nave, is divided into three bays by flattened arches on both sides of the crossing. These rest directly, without pillars or other supports, on the western wall of the transept and cross in a heavy, ungraceful way over the arcade leading from the choir and chapels to the transept. A similar example, dating from 1308, exists at the cathedral of Venzone in Italy.

Plate 83. *Saint Salvador in Canea. Franciscan monastery. Western facade.*

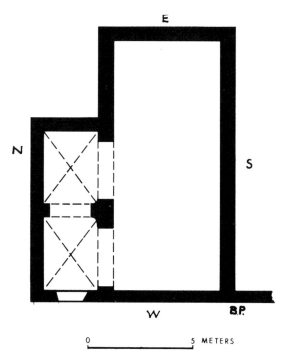

Fig. 21. *The church of Saint Salvador of Canea. Franciscan.*

To the north of the church was the monastery. Only part of its cloister survives, but at the time Gerola visited Saint Nicolas the greater part of the cloister was still in existence. Today a street crosses on the northern side of the church, and the southern gallery of the cloister has been eliminated. There still remain eight bays of the eastern gallery (FIG. 20) and two of the western one. The cloister must have been almost square, with four groin-vaulted galleries. The parts that are extant are constructed in well-cut ashlar, showing careful workmanship. The vaults rest on heavy rectangular pillars on the side facing the inner court and on the other side abut directly on the walls that sheltered the monastic buildings now destroyed.

The architecture of Saint Nicolas is another example or airiness and simplicity and of severity typical of Mediterranean monastic architecture of the Middle Ages. This church, like those in Candia, reminds one more of southern Italy than of France or Spain.

THE CHURCH OF SAINT SALVADOR IN CANEA

The smaller of the two Franciscan monasteries of Canea, less ambitious and poorer, is Saint Salvador, situated to the west of the harbor. The Turks turned it into the mosque of Ser Topu Hassan Agha. Today the church is completely abandoned and one part of it serves as a granary. The remnants of the monastery of the southern side of the church are part of a private home (PLATE 83).

The plan of the church has one small nave 13m in length, without an apse (FIG. 21). Across an arcade on the northern side, this single nave communicates with a small chapel of two bays. The church probably never had a bell tower.[63] The nave is covered by a barrel vault, and the chapel is covered by ribbed vaults that rest on corbels decorated with small flowers. A monogram of Jesus Christ is placed over the arch between the two bays of the chapel. The northern wall shows traces of two bays surmounted by pointed arches that were later eliminated. The entrance, today and according to Gerola's plan, is on the western side. A simple door surmounted by an oculus leads into the chapel, and a door surmounted by a round window seems to have led into the nave. A modern window was opened under the oculus, which was filled in and plastered over. Later both the modern window and the door of the nave were filled with rubble, leaving only the entrance through the chapel still open. It also seems that the facade on the side of the nave terminated in a gable that was later raised and squared off.

On the northern wall of the nave, where the wall extends east of the chapel, was a tomb that Gerola was able to inspect. It was constructed in the wall and surmounted by two colonnettes on which rests a sculpted archivolt.

The condition of this church today is extremely painful to see. It is, of course, small, but like many small churches it has a certain interest and should have been preserved with more care. The monastery has suffered even more from reconstructions and additions during the past two centuries, so that it is impossible even to describe it. Archeological diggings might uncover traces of its foundations. Unfortunately, we have absolutely no information on when the church and the monastery were constructed.

The Church of Saint Francis

The Franciscan church of Saint Francis in Canea, which underwent a partial restoration after World War II, is now used as the archeological museum of Canea.[64] It was the church of a monastery that is now completely destroyed. The monastery lay on the south side of the church. Gerola's plan indicates six vaulted bays,[65] of which three are now used as a shop and the other three as storerooms (FIG. 22).

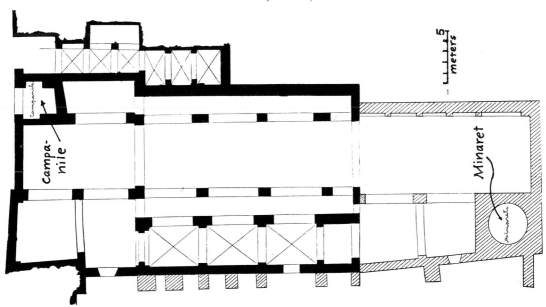

Fig. 22. *The Franciscan church of Saint Francis of Canea. Fourteenth century. Plan by Gerola.*

The church was built in the fourteenth century, but there is again no record of the exact date.[66] It was restored after the earthquake of the sixteenth century and later turned into a mosque by the Turks, who added several structures.[67] The monastery was outside the city walls of Canea in the early Venetian period but within the later Renaissance fortification of Canea in Boschini's time, as can be seen from his map of 1651 (FIG. 23), just before the Turkish occupation of the island. Boschini saw it after the restoration of the church in 1596 and the addition made in 1606.[68]

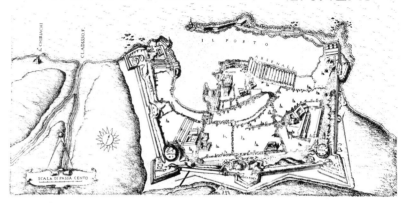

Fig. 23. *The town of Canea. Map by Boschini, seventeenth century.*

Description of the church. Nestled in the surroundings of the monastery, Saint Francis is oriented from west to east, but today one enters the church from the east side, where the street is. When Gerola visited the church there was no entrance on the east side, but there were two others (on the north and south sides), which still exist. The original entrance was from the cloister on the south side. There may also have been an entrance from the west before the Turks extended the building to the west and added a minaret on the northwest corner. The eastern windows and the door were added at the time of the Greek restoration of 1962 in what from the plan obviously was the apse.

The rectangular basilican plan of Saint Francis measures 39 m long × 19.50 m at the entrance and 18.50 m on the west side (FIG. 24). One can distinguish three stages of construction: the building program of the fourteenth century, the restoration of the sixteenth century, and finally the Turkish additions. The original basic plan of the church had a central nave and two narrow aisles like Zaraka.

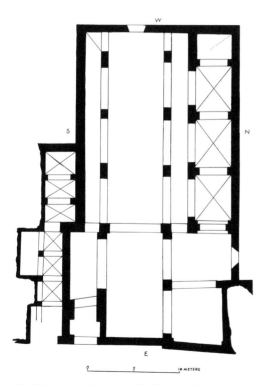

Fig. 24. *Saint Francis of Canea. Plan of the church.*

The nave ended in a flat sanctuary (FIG. 25). There are five square bays in the nave and only half a bay where the western entrance may have been. The nave is covered with a pointed barrel vault, taller than the vault over the choir and reinforced by six transverse arches resting on corbels like those of the southern chapel of Saint Peter in Candia. A band runs along the wall between the corbels (PLATE 84).

Fig. 25. Saint Francis of Canea. The bell tower, eastern view. Drawing by M. Kourouniotis and N. Sigalas.

Plate 84. Saint Francis in Canea. The nave looking west.

The aisles that communicate with the nave through an arcade are covered by half barrel vaults abutting the nave as in the church of Vlachernes in Morea (PLATE 85). These vaults are supported by half transverse arches and diaphragm arches, which at first glance strike the spectator as being the original ones, since they were covered by plaster during the restoration of 1962. They are, however, of concrete like the ones over the main nave and were added to ensure greater support of the vaults. Within these arches, two small rounded windows were opened to give a lighter effect. The aisle vaults are lower than the central nave vault.

Relying on the plan we have today, without archeological excavations, it is difficult to know whether or not the original plan had a short transept. The east side was probably restored after the 1595 earthquake, when the bell tower on the northeast side also was repaired. Its upper story was eliminated at that time, according to a letter of 1396 of Onorio Belli. The bell tower windows have tracery very closely reminiscent of fifteenth-century Venetian architecture, as for instance, the windows of the Palazzo Dandolo on the Grand Canal or the Palazzo Priuli (FIGS. 25, 26). At the base of this tower was a small chapel covered by a barrel vault, with an exit to the street. From some seventeenth-century drawings like Boschini's it appears that the tower was on the facade of the church;

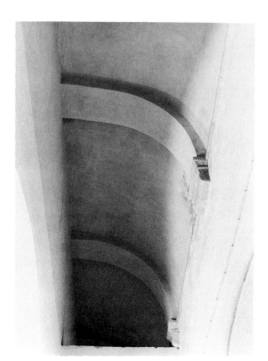

Plate 85. Saint Francis in Canea. Northern aisle vault.

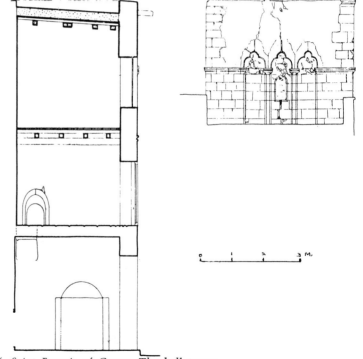

Fig. 26. Saint Francis of Canea. The bell tower, southern view. Drawing by M. Kourouniotis and N. Sigalas.

Plate 86. *Saint Francis in Canea. Northern aisle and chapels.*

however, most Italian churches have towers on the side or in the back of the church. A good sample is the Franciscan church of Santa Maria dei Frari in Venice. A round window in the east wall illuminated the choir, as can be seen in a photograph taken by Gerola before the modern restoration.

Adjacent to the choir, several chapels were added at different times. The Franciscans, as is well known, were not reluctant to add to their structures according to their occasional needs and means. They were especially forced into this because their chapter discouraged them from preaching in the churches of others. On the south side a chapel 3.50 m wide was placed behind the bell tower, which in the original plan probably stood by itself next to the choir. This chapel must certainly have been added before the cloister that leans on it was erected. It communicates with the choir and the side aisle through round arches. Two more chapels were added on the northern side of the choir, both covered with barrel vaults. The first chapel, on the northeastern corner, is of particularly uneven shape and must have been connected to the outer wall that enclosed the monastery. Both chapels communicate with each other and with the choir through arcades of round arches. The northern entrance leads through the second chapel into what is today a courtyard.

Four more chapels were added on the north side along the northern aisle. Three of them have low-domed, ribbed vaults (PLATE 86). Their ribs are carried very low down and rest on the corbels, as well as on the capitals of engaged columns decorated with delicate floral designs (PLATE 87). The arches of the arcades that lead from the chapels to the north aisle have three engaged colonnettes on the interior faces of the piers (PLATE 88). Three moldings in the form of rounded tori rest on capitals decorated in the same floral designs as the corbels (PLATE 89–92). The ribs of the vault are flattened and break into several edges, as at Saint Angelo in Orvieto (fifteenth-century) and at the Palazzo Vecchio in Florence (1299). In the center of the ribs are keystones with the monogram of Jesus Christ, as in the church of Saint Salvador in Canea (PLATE 93). The same vaulted chambers can be seen on the south side, where six bays of the cloister still exist.

Gerola's plan clearly shows an addition on the west side, made at a later date and hooked onto the main body of the church. Gerola assumes that this was added by the Turks, probably because of the exterior masonry, which without doubt is Turkish, as well as the minaret in the northwest corner.

Plate 87. *Saint Francis in Canea. Northern vaulted chapel.*

Plate 88. *Saint Francis in Canea. Capitals of the northeastern chapel.*

Plate 90. Saint Francis in Canea. Detail of capitals.

Plate 89. Saint Francis in Canea. Detail of floriated capital of a corbel.

Plate 91. Saint Francis in Canea. Detail of capitals.

Plate 92. Saint Francis in Canea. Detail of capitals.

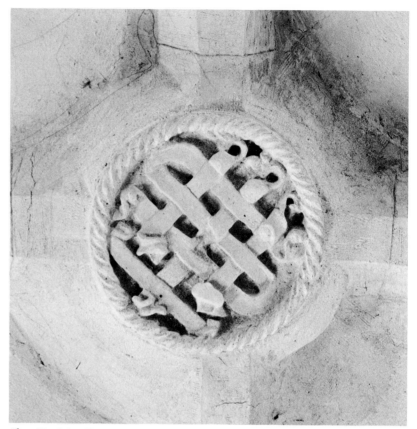

Plate 93. Saint Francis in Canea. Detail of keystone.

The inner space of this western addition, today an integral part of the remodeled museum, has consoles that do not exclude the possibility that it could have been added in the seventeenth century before the Turkish occupation. It could then have been strengthened on the outside and once more remodeled by the Turks, who added the minaret and buttresses all along the north wall. The central part of the church is not very well lighted. It gives a general feeling of a twelfth-century Cistercian church, like Fontenay, Silvanes in France, and Fossanova in Italy. It is extremely unfortunate that when the building was restored no studies were made of the original plan. The restorer relied on the plan and description of Gerola, who had seen the church cluttered by other buildings and had no opportunity to study it in depth. During the restoration the whole edifice was covered with plaster inside and out, leaving no areas where the masonry can be seen and where the additions, including the ones made in concrete in 1962, can be detected. Certainly the restoration was necessary for the preservation of the building, but just as certainly it hinders study of the church's history.

The Monastery of Bella Pais in Cyprus

Most of the Western religious orders were represented in Cyprus, as in the rest of Greece. They had settled there and on the mainland from the end of the twelfth century and the beginning of the thirteenth century, independent of their orders' other settlements in the Latin Empire. They were encouraged not only by Rome but also by the royal family of Cyprus, the Lusignans.

The Lusignans governed the island for several centuries in a more centralized manner than was usual in the other lands occupied by the Franks. As a result, the architecture of the monastic buildings of the Cypriot Middle Ages, especially between 1250 and 1350, expresses a courtly taste that in certain aspects strangely resembles the Rayonnant style of France during the same period.[69]

The supremacy of the Latin clergy was established immediately after the conquest, and Nicosia became the metropolis of the Latin archbishopric, with three dependent bishoprics: Famagusta, Limassol, and Paphos. Of all the religious orders, the Carmelites established themselves first; but no important vestige of their architecture is extant today. The Cistercians arrived in the thirteenth century almost simultaneously with their settlement in the Latin Empire.

In Nicosia, the Cistercians founded one abbey for women and another for men. The one for women, dedicated to Saint Theodore, was on the outskirts of Pyrgos in an extremely arid part of the northern coast. The other was at Beaulieu in the diocese of Nicosia. Unfortunately, neither of these abbeys exists today.

By contrast, the very beautiful monastery of Bella Pais of the Premonstratensians has survived. This order often imitated the plan of the Cistercian or Augustinian monasteries. Bella Pais, of the diocese of Nicosia, was also known as the abbey of Lapais or the White Abbey or even as the "Episcope" by the local population.

It is situated, like many Cistercian monasteries, in a magnificent landscape at the foot of a mountain near the sea south of Kyrenia, surrounded by fertile land that could be easily cultivated by the monks who settled there. Bella Pais was first inhabited by Augustinian monks, who in 1206 embraced the order of the Premonstratensians.[70] The monastery stayed in their hands until the sixteenth century, when the island was conquered by the Turks.

The greatest ravages to the abbey were caused by neighboring villages that constructed a great part of their buildings with stones taken from the monastery. Nevertheless, there remains at Bella Pais a whole group of purely Western buildings in different Gothic styles from the thirteenth to the fifteenth century.

Description of the Plan of the Monastery

The plan of the monastery forms a rectangle with the cloister in its center (PLATE 94). In the southeast rises the church, and the dormitory and refectory occupy the east and north sides (FIG. 27). In front of the church a court opens, entered through a door with crenellations and a drawbridge.

The church dates from the beginning of the thirteenth century. Construction began with the sanctuary, and the other buildings of the abbey were erected in the fourteenth century.[71]

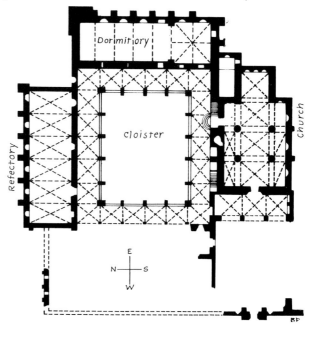

Plate 94. The monastery of Bella Pais, Cyprus. General view.

Fig. 27. Bella Pais, Cyprus. Begun in the early thirteenth century. Plan.

Plate 95. The monastery of Bella Pais. Western view of the cloister.

THE CHURCH

The plan of the church of Bella Pais is similar to the plans of other monastic churches in Greece that date from the Latin occupation. It is rectangular, ending in the east in a flat choir. The church is of average dimensions with a nave and two aisles, each with two bays and a transept not extending over the width of the church (PLATE 95). To the west, all across the facade, the building is flanked by a porch with three bays. A small chapel is placed to the east of the northern aisle, with which it does not communicate directly, and on top of this same aisle is a treasure room reached by the staircase in the wall of the second bay of the northern side aisle.

The church has three doors: one in the center of the western facade leads from the porch to the central nave; a second one on the southern side and a third also on the southern side leading from the transept to the cloister. Three windows of dimensions equal to one bay, each crowned by a pointed arch, were opened in the eastern wall of the flat sacristy, as was often done in Cistercian churches.

The elevation of the church has two stories but no triforium. An arcade of pointed arches separates the central nave from the side aisles (FIG. 28). Above it is a clerestory whose windows, like the ones that light the southern aisle, are lancets splayed both in the interior and the exterior. The whole church was vaulted with ribbed vaults, except for the southern and northern bays of the transept, which were covered by a barrel vault. The ribs of the central vault rest on the capitals of the simple round, massive columns of the nave. These columns extend into half-columns in the upper part of the nave. Their style is of the first half of the thirteenth century, and they remind one of those at Gonesse in France. A band ties these half-columns together and passes under the clerestory windows. Where the choir and the transept meet, cruciform piers with engaged thin columns rise. The ribs of the side aisles and the arcades of the nave fall on corbels against the wall, similar to those of the porch. The corbels have a rectangular plinth under which there is a basket whose base is an overturned flower.

Fig. 28. *Bella Pais, Cyprus. The nave of the church.*

The ribs of the choir have a torus that protrudes from two concave moldings. In the nave and treasury this torus is much thinner and seems to be of a more recent period. The masonry of ashlar and the details of the church of Bella Pais show very neat and careful craftsmanship.

The windows of the aisles are crowned by a beaded molding. On the west side, over the porch, a window was opened to lighten the nave even more. This window, like those on the long sides of the nave, has two frames, the second of which rests on colonnettes.

The three entrances to the church have pointed arches decorated in the same manner as these upper windows just described. The two side doors each have only one molding and two colonnettes. The one on the western facade has two moldings like voussoirs that rest on four colonnettes topped by capitals decorated with leaves and small crockets. These are common in Cistercian churches, and there are similar ones in the thirteenth century in such widely separated areas as Notre Dame de Semur en Auxois in France, Our Lady of Tortosa in the Holy Land, Zaraka, and Saint Sophia of Andravida. On mainland Greece the Attic bases with claws at the angles remind one of the bases found at Saint Nicolas of Isova, which are thirteenth century and are supposed to have come from the burned building of Our Lady of Isova.[72] They also exist in Burgundy, as well as in Italy at Casamari and at San Galgano.[73] On the west side the porch has three undecorated arcades in the form of round arches that open onto a courtyard. On the north side is another arcade in the same style, but blind, since it rests on the wall of the cloister. Four square buttresses on the west side and two more on the north and south sides stabilize the walls of the porch and of the church. The church of Bella Pais has a flat roof that has nothing Western about it but is typical of Cypriot architecture.

On the western facade over the window that looks onto the nave was a very simple bell tower with four lancet windows and a gable in the center. It must originally have ended in a pinnacle that is now destroyed.

Enlart dated the choir and the walls of the facade and aisles to the early years of the thirteenth century. The vaults of the nave and aisles were finished later, toward the middle of the century. The transept, vaulted with barrel vaults, seems even later and could have been necessitated by some accident that damaged the original structure.[74]

Generally speaking, the construction of the church, even if it was spread out over a lengthy period, looks homogeneous—certainly more so than the structures of the mendicant orders in Crete, where the monks never hesitated to make additions without considering the original plan too closely.

THE CLOISTER

The cloister was erected north of the church immediately after the church was finished. It has four bays on the western and eastern sides and seven on the other two sides (PLATE 96a, b). At the same time, the monks built a two-story building to the east of the cloister. The ground floor of the southern side was reserved for the chapter house, and the north side, which is twice as large, was used as a common work area for the monks. On the second floor a dormitory extended the whole length of the building. There was also a basement that served as a storage cellar.

Between this building and the apse of the church was the single-nave chapel already mentioned. Since the cloister was all vaulted with ribbed vaults, corbels were placed on both the wall of the above-mentioned building to the east and on the church.

The cloister wall on the west side is now in ruins and it is difficult to know what kind of building existed. Probably it housed on the first floor a kitchen and stables, and on the upper floor a hall for the novices.[75] To the north the cloister is attached to the refectory. The sculptural decorations of the corbels of the cloister are among the most beautiful of the Latin Orient. Their naturalistic foliage belongs to the second half of the thirteenth century and has parallels in Champagne. Among the sculpture of these corbels are a few human figures, as on the corbel of the choir of Saint Sophia in Andravida, but of a later style. In the second half of the thirteenth century the profiles of the sculptural ornamentation become narrower and grow more and more lacy. The foliage, which until that time had been stylized, became more ornate and had naturalistic leaves and figures.[76]

The vaults of the cloister were added at the beginning of the fourteenth century, judging from the profile of their ribs, which are more complicated than the ribs of the church. In the center of the crossings of the ribs are circular keystones decorated with foliage similar to the decorations of the corbels of the north side of the cloister. The keystone of the last western bay of the northern and southern galleries has the coat of arms of the Lusignan family.

The arcades of the cloister rest on the side facing the court on colonnettes tied together by a molding. Their capitals are also decorated by foliage. In the arches one can still see fragments of flowing, lacy tracery forming delicate foils and cusps.

Plate 96. The monastery of Bella Pais. The cloister: (a) east side; (b) west side.

Plate 97. The monastery of Bella Pais. The refectory.

THE REFECTORY

The most extraordinary building of Bella Pais is the refectory, one of the biggest and most beautiful anywhere, including the West (PLATE 97). We have no other extant refectory of Latin monks in Greece. It forms a rectangle 30.40m × 10.04m and measures 11.50m in height. It has six bays covered by ribbed vaulting. The ribs are carried by engaged colonnettes in the wall and grouped in bunches, as they are on the interior side of the cloister and the colonnettes are crowned by capitals with very lacy foliage.

On the northern facade, five completely vertical buttresses hold the wall up to the terrace, and two larger ones are placed at the corners. There are two more on the western side. The southern wall was held up by the gallery of the cloister.

The refectory hall is lighted by a small rose window on the east side and by a two-light window with a pointed arch on the west side (PLATE 107). On the northern side, every bay has two windows, one placed very low in the wall and the other, much smaller, placed very high. The last bay on the east side has a two-light window just like the one on the west. On the southern side there is a row of small windows high up in the wall and only two lower down, which look onto the cloister. The refectory communicates with the cloister by two doors. On the southwestern side is a beautiful doorway with a pointed arch decorated with a chevron motif. The archivolt, in the form of a dripstone, has a diamond pattern. Two small columns on each side of the door have floriated capitals in a style characteristic of the second half of the twelfth century. The tympanum is decorated with three blind arches, and on the marble lintel are three Lusignan coats of arms.

In the interior of the refectory and in the fifth bay, about midway from the floor, is a beautiful pulpit incorporated within the wall, richly sculpted with trefoils and quatrefoils. Light is shed on the pulpit from a traceried lancet window behind it.

The staircase of the pulpit is incorporated within the thickness of the wall and is invisible from the hall below. This building closely resembles the architecture of the end of the thirteenth century or the beginning of the fourteenth century in the south of France and Catalonia. Below the refectory hall is a large crypt that served as a cellar. It had two aisles with three bays each, separated by short octagonal columns and was lighted by very small windows placed exactly under those of the refectory. These columns carry ribbed vaults and have transverse arches with flattened angular ribs. The ribs rest on polygonal, smooth corbels and capitals. These angular flat ribs resemble those of the large hall of the monastery of Val-buena or the abbey of the Poblet in Spain, which date from the first half of the thirteenth century and have ribs with rectangular profiles. The kitchen, now destroyed, was on the west side and led to the refectory through the cellar.

THE BUILDING ON THE EAST SIDE

The large building on the east was vaulted on each of its three floors. It was started in 1325 at the same time as the cloister and the chapel between the church and the chapter house. From this building one can directly enter the church and the cloister but not the chapter house. The chapter house was a square room with a central column from which sprang the ribs of four vaults, as was the practice in the west. These vaults were ruined in the seventeenth century, and the columns also no longer exist.[77] The corbels, however, were very carefully rendered in drawings by Enlart.[78] They carry figurines of the fourteenth century.

THE WORKROOM OF THE MONKS

To the north of the chapter house, as part of the building on the east side, was the work hall of the monks. It had five bays vaulted with a barrel vault. Remnants of it can still be seen. The transverse arches that supported the vault rested on corbels crowned by a simple plinth.

Rows of windows on the eastern and western sides let light into this hall, and a door led to the cloister. On the north side another door, above which was a round window, opened onto a balcony that has now been destroyed but whose location still gives a breathtaking view of the valley of Kyrenia.

THE DORMITORY

Above the chapter house and the study hall is the dormitory, also partially destroyed, though the general plan can still be discerned (PLATE 98). It has only one nave of seven bays covered by ribbed vaults. The vaults, now in ruins, were carried by half-columns engaged in the walls. The columns were crowned by foliated octagonal capitals similar to those of the cloister and the refectory (PLATE 99). At the angles of the dormitory the vaults were supported by corbels richly ornamented with flowers and leaves.

Here too a small window corresponds with every bay, and there was also a small closet for each monk. On the north side, exactly above the door of the study hall balcony, was a large pointed, mullioned window with flowing tracery. A small passage covered by a ribbed vault, placed in the southern wall of the dormitory, leads to a stone staircase that takes one up to the terrace and down to the portal leading from the cloister to the church. From there different staircases lead to the treasure chamber or to the terrace above the church.

Plate 98. The monastery of Bella Pais. Undercroft and dormitory.

The vaults of the small passage in the wall of the dormitory were supported by sculptured corbels. The only one that remains represents a nude woman fighting against a monster. Enlart dates this corbel in the fourteenth century.[79]

An exterior wall protected the abbey of Bella Pais on the southern and western sides. The northern and eastern sides needed no wall because of the enormous steepness of the rock on which the monastery is built. The main entrance was through the western enceinte, over a drawbridge and an impressive gateway with crenellations facing the church.

Bella Pais has no parallel in Greece. The monastery enjoyed the gifts and protection of the Lusignans, and its rich decorations seem contrary to the spirit of the monastic orders who lived in it. Only the plan of the church reminds one of the Latin churches in Greece. The ample space, particularly in the refectory and its cellar, recalls southern France and Spain. The sculptural ornamentation is homogeneous even though it was completed over a long period of time, and one sees coordination in the ornamentation of the windows and capitals and archivolts throughout the buildings, especially in the areas executed between 1250 and 1350.

Plate 99. *The monastery of Bella Pais. Details of the dormitory.*

The most striking effect is the contrast between the monumental buildings and the fragile decor, between the mural massiveness and the laciness of the traceried windows and arcades. This phenomenon is unique not to Cyprus but rather to this period of Gothic art, which begins with the Rayonnant style in the middle of the thirteenth century.

This style was initiated in the West through courtly patronage of the arts and has been called the "courtly style."[80] Under its influence, buildings as delicate as Sainte Chapelle were created, but so were monumental structures exemplified by the palace of the popes of Avignon.

Saint Louis represents the best example of a courtly patron. He not only created a workshop at his own court but also patronized the Mendicants, Dominicans, Franciscans, and the order of the Carmelites after his return from the Holy Land.[81] Above all, he encouraged the construction of monasteries at the expense of the court. In the same spirit, the Lusignans were to a great extent responsible for the architecture of the abbey of Bella Pais and other monasteries of Cyprus.

According to a traveler, Bella Pais was already in ruins in 1560.[82] The Latin monks were expelled by the Turks a little later, and the monastery suffered greatly from the local people, who used its stones for their own construction.

Saint Francis of Famagusta: A Franciscan Church

The Franciscan church of Saint Francis at Famagusta was probably built by Henry II between 1284 and 1324. It is largely in ruins today, but its general plan is still visible. It had a single nave 12 m × 9 m, with three bays that ended in a polygonal sanctuary (FIG. 34a) 10 m in length. It has been speculated that in the fifteenth century two chapels were added, to the north and south. The one to the north has been completely destroyed but the southern one is well preserved. According to Enlart it is very probable that there never was a northern chapel because it is on that side that the cloister was attached to the church.[83] On each side of the second bay of the nave an arcade was added that communicated with the chapels, which had the length of one bay of the nave but were not as large or as tall. These chapels formed a sort of transept to the west of the church.

The church had no towers, which was quite normal for the church of a Franciscan monastery, where the rule was "Campanile ecclesiae ad modum turris de caetero nusquam fiat."[84]

The interior of the church was covered by ribbed vaults. These ribs and formerets rested on overturned pyramidal corbels naturalistically decorated with foliage as at Bella Pais. They date from about 1300. The ribs had a profile of three tori next to each other, with a cavetto on each side.

The southern chapel is covered by a ribbed vault that rests on four colonnettes with round capitals, like the ones on the windows but with more ornate foliage. The profile of these ribs is different from those of the nave. There are deep concave grooves on both sides of the torus, followed by countercurves and half-flat projections. These ribs are of a more advanced style, which indicates that at least the southern chapel was added much later. They remind one of the ribs of the cathedral of Nevers or of Saint Benigne at Dijon.

The windows of the church are rather large; their pointed arches are supported on the inner side by colonnettes with foliated capitals. The exterior face of these arches is crowned by archivolts. There are still five such windows in the polygonal sanctuary wall, which date from about the thirteenth century. The southern wall has two large openings in the masonry, one between the apse and the existing chapel and the other between the chapel and the western facade. The northern side is completely destroyed. The southern chapel is lighted on the south side by a lancet window crowned by a double design on the inner side and a triple design on the outer. Of the western portal nothing is extant except one jamb decorated with a molding. East and west are two round windows with a geometric foil tracery resembling that of the portal of Saint Urbain at Troyes.

The apse is reinforced by six vertical buttresses that continue straight up to the top of the wall. Like Bella Pais, the church of Saint Francis, especially in its plan and its spaciousness, reminds one of the art of southern France.

The monastery, of which only a part of the facade still survives, lay to the north and west of the church. To the south rose the royal palace; a direct but secret passage led to it from the monastery and church.[85]

We know from the description of a traveler in 1394 that the monastery had a beautiful cloister, a dormitory, several other rooms, an attractive garden, and many wells and cisterns.[86] Today it is impossible to know exactly where those buildings were. Enlart, in fact, suggests that instead of a monastery, there might have been a Genoese loggia on the northern side.[87] It seems rather improbable that we will ever have the true answer to these speculations.

Part Three   OTHER CHURCH ARCHITECTURE

5 Parochial Churches

The Church of Saint Paraskevi at Chalkis—Euboea

Very few parochial Latin churches in Greece have survived. Most were used by monastic orders that received their support from the Holy See. The Latin communities were not so numerous in each region as to require several parochial churches, and the Greek population preferred Orthodox churches.

The few Latin churches that are extant show conclusively the similarities between the parochial and monastic churches and their preference for a flat, rectangular eastern sanctuary. This must not be interpreted only as the reflection of a poor community, since such sanctuaries appear not only in Greece but also in the West, in Catalonia, and in the Balearic Islands, where the monastic orders exercised considerable influence on the architecture of the thirteenth and fourteenth centuries.[1]

The church of Saint Paraskevi, as it is called today, must certainly have been named differently by the Franks, who latinized even the names of Byzantine churches they occupied. It has been proposed that it could have been named for the Virgin, since there already existed before the Latin conquest a church of the Virgin named "Theotokos Perivleptos" that could have been Saint Paraskevi.[2] An inscription that mentions the church of the Virgin is now kept in the museum of Chalkis, but was discovered in the courtyard of another church not far from Saint Paraskevi.[3] In addition to all this, according to the chronicle, Henri de Valenciennes visited the church of the Virgin in 1205 when the town of Chalkis gave itself up to Jacques d'Avesnes.

The important town of Chalkis, which sheltered within its walls the church of Saint Paraskevi, was also known as Negreponte during the Latin occupation. Even before the conquest it had been the seat of an Orthodox diocese, and after 1260, when Constantinople was returned to the hands of the Byzantines, Negreponte became the seat of a Latin patriarchate. Because of its military and commercial importance, the Venetian part of the town was fortified in 1303 by Francesco Dandolo, as can be seen on the map and engraving of Coronelli.[4] The emblem of Saint Mark that can still be seen in the museum of the town was placed over the main entrance. Only traces of these walls are in existence today. The Turkish conquest by Mohammed II in 1470 destroyed a large part of the town. Negreponte certainly had more than one Latin church, but the church of Saint Paraskevi, almost everyone agrees, played a most important role. According to J. Koder, it was not a parish church but a cathedral.[5] He believes that after 1261, when Contantinople was again in Greek hands and a Latin patriarch had his seat in Negreponte, this was the church facing the patriarch's residence.

If that is true, this residence, still in existence, is wrongly called by the people of Chalkis the palace of the Venetian bailie. Over its doorway is another symbol of Saint Mark, but its facade is in the Renaissance style of the fifteenth century, a later date than that of Saint Paraskevi.

No one has doubted the importance of the church of Saint Paraskevi, but some scholars have contended that as the seat of the Latin bishop it was called Saint Mark and was directly related to San Giorgio Maggiore of Venice. But in his recent study Koder suggests that Saint Mark was situated where today there is a mosque, on the neighboring square not far from the church of Saint Paraskevi. The church of Saint Mark was built during the early years of the Frankish occupation of Negreponte, for its name appears in the testament of Pietro da Famo in June 1215 and is also documented in the correspondence between Marino and Ricardo dalle Carceri of 1216. Turkish descriptions strengthen this view. According to Koder, next to the church of Saint Mark was the Venetian loggia and, on the same square, the palace of the bailie. The loggia and the palace were built at the same time, but not before 1273. Only after that date are both of these buildings mentioned in different documents: the loggia alone in a document of 1281, and both several times after 1400, when all sorts of repairs were made in 1403, 1409, 1410, 1413, 1417, 1419, and 1421.[6]

The assumption that the church of Saint Mark was next to the loggia on the central square of the fortified town is very plausible. The same arrangement can still be seen in Herakleion in Crete, where the church of Saint Mark that had been preserved was across from the ducal palace and next to the loggia, which is now being reconstructed. Also, like the church of Saint Mark in Crete, the church of Saint Mark in Negreponte was directly under the ecclesiastical rule of Venice and San Giorgio Maggiore rather than under the local bishop. Of course it would be necessary to excavate the mosque for further proof, but this seems a logical interpretation of the known documents.

Besides the church of Saint Mark and the church of the Virgin visited by Henri de Valenciennes in 1205 (which probably refers to Saint Paraskevi), there is also mention from the beginning of the thirteenth century of a monastic church of the Virgin and of a hospital of the Italian order of the Crociferi. In 1223, Pope Honorius III wrote a letter mentioning the hospital to the brothers of the order in Negreponte.[7] The church of the Virgin of the Crociferi is again mentioned in documents of 1256 and 1262 as Sancta Maria Crociferorum, which indicates that the order was still active in Negreponte up to that date.

Even though the church of Saint Paraskevi has been considered until now a parochial church—or a cathedral, according to Koder —it seems probable that since it was named for the Virgin (coinciding with the name of the church of the Virgin of the Crociferi), it may be the same church. This building may have been at first given to the order of the Crociferi, who remodeled it in a style already found in all of the other churches of the mendicant orders in Greece. The location of Saint Paraskevi within the walled city and near the church of Saint Mark and the Venetian governmental center is similar to the location of Saint Mary of the Crusaders (Crociferi) in Herakleion in Crete.

Of the other orders, we only have some written information. It is known that there was a monastery of Saint Francis and that at the beginning of the thirteenth century the "Canonici Dominici Templi" had a church of Saint Nicolas de Negreponte.[8]

DESCRIPTION OF THE CHURCH

The plan of Saint Paraskevi is basilican, 37m in length, with a nave and two aisles. The nave ends in a flat sanctuary and the aisles in square chapels without apses.

On the same site where Saint Paraskevi now stands, there had been a Byzantine church from the end of the fifth century or the beginning of the sixth. There are still remnants of the columns and capitals,[9] some of which have naturalistic acanthus leaves. Changes must have been brought about between this period and the thirteenth century, for fragments were found of a lintel that Xyngo-poulos dates to the eleventh century and that, according to him, replaced a more ancient one.[10]

The church was probably destroyed at the time of the Frankish occupation in the thirteenth century.[11] It was rebuilt and various changes and additions were made to its plan and elevation. The columns of the ancient basilica were retained and their bases placed on today's pavement. The foundations also came from the ancient church, for the proportions of the nave and aisles are not different from those of the Byzantine basilica.[12]

The western facade was reconstructed after the earthquake of 1853. It must have been placed a little farther back, for there still remain in front of the church two columns whose capitals are Byzantine, with small Ionic volutes surmounted by a truncated pyramid and ornamented by a circular monogram (PLATE 100).

Plate 100. *Saint Paraskevi in Chalkis. Western facade.*

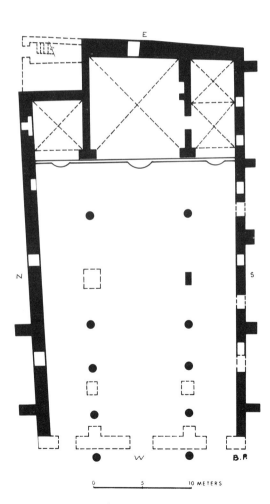

Fig. 29. Saint Paraskevi, Chalkis. Thirteenth century. Plan of the church.

In the interior, two rectangular piers were placed between the columns of the last arcade during the last reconstruction. They carry an upper gallery (PLATE 101). It is clear that before this new addition, the nave was separated from the aisles by an arcade of four arches, one of which has now been eliminated; on each side one of the columns is, for this reason, still standing on the outside of the church (FIG. 29). Over this arcade are four bays: three have

Plate 101. Saint Paraskevi. Northwestern elevation seen from the nave.

pointed arches and the fourth has a round arch. They give the impression that there was a gallery behind them that has now disappeared. Certain observations prove its existence: one can still see the traces of four windows above the southern aisle, though they have now been blocked. These windows correspond exactly to the bays placed over the arcade and must have lighted the gallery. The piers between the bays are ornamented by a flat, simple band. A stringcourse continues around the nave right above the arches.

The arcade that separates the central nave from the aisle stops at approximately two-thirds of the length of the nave, against a rectangular pier. From this point on there is another arcade with two taller and larger pointed arches (PLATE 102), both resting on one central Byzantine column.

At this point of the nave the upper gallery terminates (PLATE 103). It is possible that this central part of the church was less damaged and retains more of the eleventh-century Byzantine church.

The wall is finished off by a cornice with corbels ornamented with a Frankish coat of arms. At this point the open-beam pointed roof merges with the wall (PLATE 104).[13] This roof dates from the thirteenth century Western church and has several parallels in Western Europe as well as at Isova in the Peloponnesus. It seems curious that windows were not opened to light the central nave more. Nevertheless, the nave is not very dark; its light comes from the six windows of the aisles. These aisles are covered by an inclined wooden roof.

Besides the three modernized doors of the western facade, the church had three more entrances on the southern side. These three southern doors, which have now been closed off, were placed so that each led into one bay of the aisle. Each had a lintel across the top, over which there was a pointed relieving arch enclosing a flat, empty tympanum. It is difficult to imagine why so many doors were necessary, especially if Saint Paraskevi did not belong to a monastery. These doors are placed much lower than today's ground level. In the church the pavement is half a meter higher than before.

On the outside the basilica was supported on the south by four buttresses and on the north by only two. These buttresses, larger at the base and tapering to a narrower top, were not part of the original building. In the interior, the nave and aisles lead into the choir and chapels through three pointed arches. The central one has a diaphragm arch (PLATE 105). All the arches of the church are very simple, with a flat band that emphasizes the openings, except the one over the choir, which is ornamented with foliage.

Plate 102. Saint Paraskevi. The southern aisle seen from the choir.

Plate 103. Saint Paraskevi. Arcade between the nave and the northern aisle.

Plate 104. Saint Paraskevi. Open-beam wooden roof over the nave.

Plate 105. Saint Paraskevi. Triumphal arch of the choir.

The choir forms an almost exact square, each side being 8 m except the northern side, which is slightly longer. It is covered by a groin vault. The northern chapel did not communicate with the choir at the time Traquair visited it,[14] but today there is a modern door.

This chapel is also square (5 m × 5 m), covered by a ribbed vault, slightly domed. The ribs are round and massive, with an archaic appearance. They seem to have been added as a decoration rather than incorporated from the start to reinforce the vault. These ribs rest on very elongated corbels, richly decorated with a lacy ornament that must be dated to the fourteenth century. The work is not very carefully executed.

The southern chapel leads directly to the choir. It has two bays and is covered by a ribbed vault (PLATE 106). The ribs are lighter and form simple tori projecting from a band; the keystones represent lion's heads and small crowns of foliage (PLATE 108), and in the center of the arch band there is a cluster of grapevines.

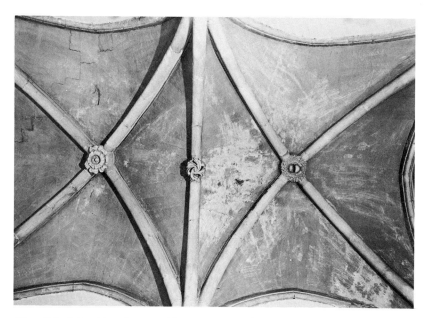

Plate 106. Saint Paraskevi. Ribbed vault of the southern chapel.

Plate 107. Saint Paraskevi. Detail of the keystone of the southern chapel.

Plate 108. Saint Paraskevi. Detail of the keystone of the southern chapel.

The ribs, like those at Saint Sophia of Andravida, do not rest directly on the corbels but first gather onto the corbeling, which in turn sits on a corbel ornamented with very lacy foliage (PLATE 110). These corbels strongly resemble those of the cloister of Bella Pais and must date from the end of the thirteenth century. They represent leaves of vine, oak, and poplar and are as finely sculpted as the keystones (plates 110, 111, 112, 113).

Plate 109. Saint Paraskevi. Southern chapel seen from behind the iconostasis.

Plate 110. Saint Paraskevi. Detail of the northern corbel of the southern chapel.

Plate 111. Saint Paraskevi. Detail of corbel in the southwest corner of the southern chapel.

Plate 112. *Saint Paraskevi. Detail of corbel in the northeast corner of the southern chapel.*

Plate 114. *Saint Paraskevi. Southern wall of the southern chapel.*

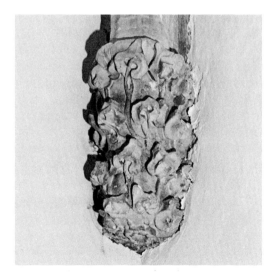

Plate 113. *Saint Paraskevi. Detail of corbel in the southeast corner of the southern chapel.*

A pointed arch with an archivolt opening within a rectangular slab was placed in front of one of the imposts of the southern side of the chapel (PLATE 114). This architectural unit was brought over from a later monument after the southern chapel was finished and was placed against the wall so as to frame its square window.

A small niche in the southern wall of the choir was used as a piscina. Its exterior frame forms a pointed arch, and the interior is trilobed.

The western wall of the choir incorporates three windows in the upper part of the wall and one a little lower down. These three windows and the square east end were interpreted by Enlart as influences from the Champagne area of France.[15] The southern chapel has no windows on the east side.

At the angle of the choir and the northern chapel a modern bell tower was erected in 1927. It is probable that the fourth window of the choir not mentioned by Enlart also was added then. This bell tower replaced another destroyed before the earthquake of 1853, which is mentioned by Didron.

Inside the northern chapel, which is lighted by only one window on the northern side, is another niche with a slightly later inscription. This niche belongs to the tomb of a Petrus Lipamanus, who died in 1398. The little statue of the Virgin placed next to it is Byzantine of the fifteenth century.[16]

Today the church is used for the Greek Orthodox liturgy and an iconostasis was added between the choir, the chapels, and the naves and aisles. Since women are not allowed behind the iconostasis, I could not observe it firsthand and had to rely on someone else's description of the inner sanctum.

Except for the Western part, the church of Saint Paraskevi is Gothic, built over the foundations of the Byzantine church. It was probably built in the thirteenth century, before 1279. The southern chapel with its ornamented corbels indicated French influence, possibly that of Champagne. The northern chapel was built somewhat later, in the fourteenth century, and was probably executed by Greek workers. Its corbels are according to Venetian taste.

The spaciousness and the simplicity of the greater part of the church is similar to that of monastic churches, especially those of the mendicant orders of Crete, and also reminds one of southern France and Italy. However, the masterworkers here had to be constantly aware of the proportions and foundations of the earlier structures preceding the thirteenth-century Gothic church.

The Church of Saint Mark of Candia in Crete
The church of Saint Mark in Candia was certainly the symbol of Venice in Crete, in contrast to Saint Paraskevi or the church of the Virgin.

Saint Mark was built in the center of the fortified town (FIG. 30)[17] on the eastern side of the square of Saint Mark and did not depend on the Latin archbishopric of Crete, whose cathedral was the ancient Byzantine church of Saint Titus. It was the church of the dukes of Candia and was managed by a *primacerio* appointed directly by the duke.

In this building the dukes of the kingdom of Crete not only prayed but were buried. Several sarophagi and tomb plaques decorated with sculptural ornaments testify to this practice. Some of them are kept today in the historical museum of Herakleion (Candia).

The construction of Saint Mark establishes the independence of Venice, even in church affairs, from the authority of the pope, as well as announcing the intention of the Venetian colonizers to create in this new homeland a smaller Venice. All official ceremonies were sanctified here, and religious sentiment mingled with the patriotism of these Venetians for the *Dominante.*[18]

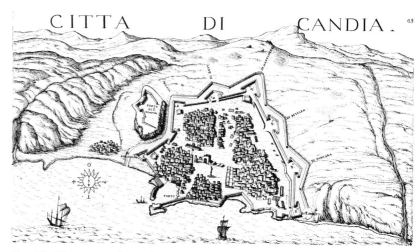

Fig. 30. The town of Candia. Drawing by Bos-chini.

The construction of the church of Saint Mark must have begun a little after 1239, for on 5 July 1239 Pope Gregory IX, in a letter to the bishop of Jerapetra, gave permission for the erection of a church dedicated to Saint Mark the Evangelist.[19] Very shortly afterward, the bishop of Jerapetra placed the first stone, and the church was completed in 1244, when Duke Tommaso Duado procured the adjoining land for the bell tower and the cemetery. The history of the church after the end of the thirteenth century is very complicated.

In 1303, on 8 August, an earthquake not only destroyed many sections of Candia but also caused catastrophies in a large part of the island and almost completely destroyed the church of Saint Mark. Requests were being submitted as early as 1306, but it was only in 1336 that the church was finally reconstructed.

Unfortunately, in 1508 another serious earthquake shook the church and the bell tower. They were repaired, but probably not as well as they should have been, for in the years 1549, 1552, and 1557 there was continual talk about the necessary 800 ducats demanded from Venice for repairs to Saint Mark. Finally the tower was repaired from the revenues of the church, but on 24 August 1564, another earthquake destroyed the facade, and on 17 November 1595 still another disastrously shook the southern part of the church. In 1599 the chief master mason Michael Raftopoulos and the chief carpenter John Clados, who were called to inspect the church, decided to reinforce certain parts.

During the war against the Turks, which lasted twenty-four years, from 1645 to 1669, the church suffered again, this time from bombardments.[20] The Turks transformed Saint Mark into a mosque and demolished the bell tower, replacing it with a minaret. The paintings of the church were completely destroyed.[21] When Gerola visited Saint Mark it was still a mosque. In 1956 it was reconstructed in an effort to recreate the church that was there before the Turkish occupation. Again, the whole church was covered with stucco and whitewashed so that no examination of the masonry is possible. The building is used today as an exhibition hall of the town of Herakleion.

Plate 115. *Saint Mark of Candia. The nave, view from the east about 1239.*

DESCRIPTION OF THE CHURCH

The plan of Saint Mark is extremely simple and very spacious. It is a rectangle divided into two aisles and a nave, the nave slightly larger than the aisles (PLATE 115). The exterior dimensions are 33.95m × 17.60m. The central nave measures 6.60m, the southern

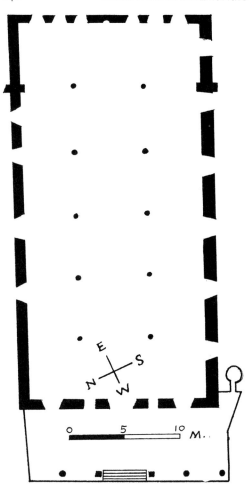

Fig. 31. Saint Mark of Candia. A.D. *1239. Plan of the church.*

aisle 4.60m, and the northern aisle 4.40m. The porch, or "loggia" as the Venetians called it, projected 6.15m over the western side (FIG. 31). The nave was separated from the aisles by two pointed arcades that rested on columns whose cubical capitals were probably extremely simple. Only those of the last bay before the sanctuary are more ornate, with very naturalistic leaves. They originally belonged to the church that was rebuilt after the earthquake of 1303. One of the bases of the columns was made from an overturned capital.

The supports of the roof must have come from different sources[22] and were not all of the same height. This was also a primary cause for the instability of the buildings. Certain columns of green stone must have come from Roman structures in Candia or Cnossos.[23] The bases of the columns, apart from the overturned capital, are very simple, cubical and covered with mortar bearing very schematic acanthus leaves. The choir is not separated from the rest of the church by an arcade in the usual way. There is only a low platform on which the altar was placed.

The nave must have been higher than the side aisles, both aisles and nave were covered by slightly inclined roofs (FIG. 32). Also, there must have been clerestory windows over the arcades in the center of the church.[24] Today, however, the nave and the aisles are of almost equal height. In the course of the Turkish occupation, the height of the nave was probably lowered, and the whole church was covered with an inclined roof of only two sides placed on a sharply pointed gable. The pavement of the church is made of diagonally placed plaques of local stone. Only the doors of the western and northern facades are original. The western one was rebuilt according to the one seen on Corner's design (FIG. 33). During the Turkish occupation, several other doors were opened: two in the western side and another in the eastern side. There are only five pointed windows as reminders of the Venetian period, placed quite high in the southern wall (PLATE 116). There must surely have been another five at the same height on the northern side. The east end had six windows before the restoration, but today there are only four. It seems quite probable, however, that the original church had six windows that allowed more light into the church and dramatized the sanctuary. Under the western and eastern gables there probably were two more windows that lighted the nave along with the clerestory windows. The walls were covered with murals just like Saint Peter and Saint Mary of the Crusaders, but these were all destroyed by the Turks.

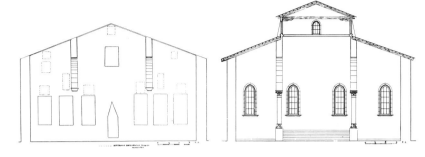

Fig. 32. Saint Mark of Candia before and after the restoration. The sanctuary wall. Drawings by St. Alexiou and K. Lassithiotakis.

Fig. 33. Allegorical figure of Candia holding the church of Saint Mark.

Plate 116. Saint Mark of Candia. The nave, view toward the altar.

After the earthquake of 1564 that destroyed the western facade, a porch was added all along the new facade, strongly reminiscent of the Italian porches of the Renaissance (FIG. 32). It was covered by a flat roof resting on an arcade composed of five round arches directly supported by columns with fourteenth-century capitals. Today only three of the original columns are left. This porch later suffered from the changes made by the Turks, who had no feeling for Renaissance balance and destroyed the arcades, placing a sloping roof directly on the capitals. The principal entrance, topped by a lintel and a round relieving arch, must date from the same period.

In 1552, when the church had to be stabilized, a report was presented to the duke mentioning the necessity of constructing four buttresses on the northern side.[25] But only two were built, which still exist.

The bell tower was built on the south side, separate from the church building, according to the Italian habit. It had a flat roof ending in crenellations and carried a clock.

Plate 117. Santa Croce, Florence, 1294. The nave.

Plate 118. Saint Mark of Candia. Western facade.

THE CHURCH OF SAINT GEORGE OF THE LATINS IN CYPRUS

The most ancient parochial church of the town of Famagusta was Saint George of the Latins (probably called this to differentiate it from Saint George of the Greeks in Famagusta). Today, as when

Enlart studied the churches of Cyprus,[26] only the northern wall and a part of the eastern sanctuary still exist, together with part of the corbeling on the southern side. It would be impossible to restore the building today, not only because of the very difficult political situation in Cyprus since 1974, but also because all the stones were taken away by local inhabitants for use in their own structures. Restoration would actually mean reconstruction with mostly new materials (PLATE 120).

Plate 119. *Saint Mark of Candia. Door in the northern wall.*

Plate 120. *Saint George of the Latins, Famagusta: Built 1248. Northeastern side.*

According to Francis, Saint George was constructed before 1248, a short time before the visit to Famagusta of Saint Louis, king of France.[27] Enlart places it a little later, toward the last quarter of the thirteenth century or the beginning of the fourteenth.

Its plan is that of a basilica, with a single nave divided into four bays that end in a polygonal apse (FIG. 34*b*). North of the choir is a low square vestry covered by a groin vault. The rest of the church had ribbed vaults resting on corbeling that are vaguely reminiscent of Saint Sophia of Andravida and Saint Paraskevi at Chalkis. This corbeling was supported by clusters of three small pillars. The pro-

Plate 121. Saint George of the Latins. South-western view.

files of the ribs had almond-shaped tori bordered on each side by cavetti.

Saint George is lighted by long narrow windows all along the walls and between the rectangular perpendicular buttresses on the outside. These pointed windows take up two-thirds of the height of the walls. They remind one strongly of the windows of the Sainte Chapelle in Paris. They have an exterior and an interior embrasure in the Western manner and were divided by a mullion whose traces can still be seen. Unfortunately, we cannot recreate the designs of the tracery, since there are absolutely no vestiges. They were probably composed of trefoils as on the northern portal, where roses and quatrefoils can be seen (PLATE 121). The windows have the traditional shape of Rayonnant art in the West. Saint George is one of the best examples of this style in Cyprus.

On each jamb of the windows one can still see the colonnettes that probably supported the arcading, with the tracery above. The capitals of these colonnettes, as well as those that support the ribs of the vaults, have a floriated naturalistic style. On certain capitals winged monsters with two bodies appear. They are reminiscent of Romanesque work, but their style is more dynamic and the workmanship of the stone is lacier.

The church must have had three portals. One would have been to the west, but it has disappeared along with the whole facade except for the northern corner. The others were on each side of the second bay. Only the one on the northern side exists today. This portal is crowned by pointed voussoirs and a sharply pointed pediment that encloses a trefoil with pointed lobes. The capitals of the columns that support the archivolts are decorated with naturalistic foliage in the same manner as in the interior of the church.

At the northern angle, the only survival of the western facade, one can see a small spiral staircase. According to an engraving done by a certain Stefano Gibellino, there must have been a similar staircase on the southern side of the western facade, which led to a bell tower taller than the church itself.[28]

The tower on the northwestern side, however, was not taller than the facade. Part of the cantilever construction of this tower still exists. It is ornamented with floral and interlaced animal motifs; for instance, a scene of a lion strangling a donkey. The style is the same as in the treatment of the foliage, but the subject matter, which can also be found in the West, strongly reminds one of ancient themes on Near Eastern patterns.

In the upper part of the projecting buttresses, under a triangular abutment, are sculptured gargoyles in a very fine style that could be compared with those of Saint Urbain of Troyes in France.[29] In the interior of the church, along the northern wall, one can still see tombs built within the thickness of the wall, crowned by pointed arches. The whole church was covered by a terrace ending in crenellations.

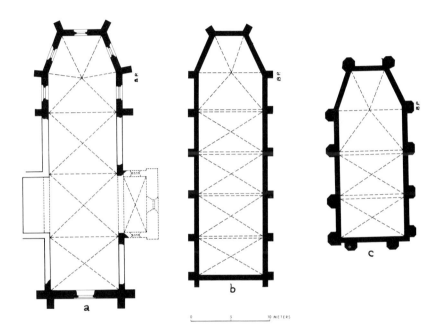

Fig. 34. Comparisons of plans of Gothic churches on Cyprus: (a) Saint Francis of Famagusta; (b) Saint George of the Latins, Famagusta; (c) Saint Catherine of Nicosia.

Saint George has a great deal in common with the other Latin churches of Cyprus (FIG. 34). Its architectural style is much more elaborate and richer than that of Greece and is more directly influenced by examples of courtly art of the Rayonnant style built in northern France from the middle of the thirteenth century. The single nave, its two-story elevation, and its polygonal apse, however, are not unrelated to the plans of the churches in Greece we have mentioned (FIG. 35). What is characteristic of Saint George of the Latins is the thinning down of the walls, the dissolution of the surfaces, and the lack of interest in mural quality that is so striking in the churches of mainland Greece and especially Crete (FIG. 36).

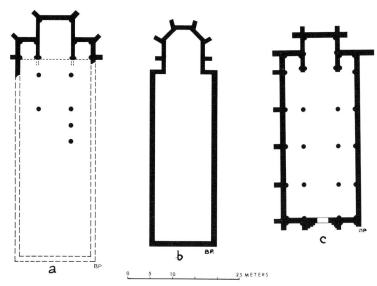

Fig. 35. Comparative plans of the churches of (a) Andravida, (b) Our Lady of Isova; and (c) Zaraka.

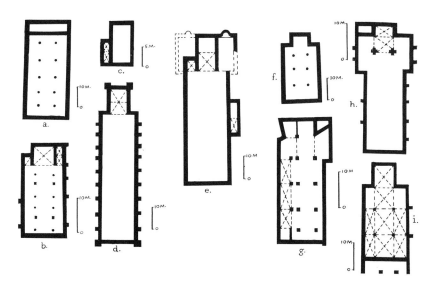

Fig. 36. Other plans of Gothic churches in Greece: (a) Saint Mark of Candia; (b) Saint Paraskevi, Chalkis; (c) Saint Salvador, Canea; (d) Saint Salvador, Candia; (e) Saint Peter Martyr, Candia; (f) Saint Mary of the Crusaders; (g) Saint Francis of Canea; (h) Saint Nicolas of Canea; (i) Bella Pais, Cyprus.

Another purely Gothic example of northern French architecture in Cyprus is Saint Catherine of Nicosia, which we must not omit from this study. Built a little more recently than Saint George of the Latins, it dates from the end of the fourteenth century (PLATE 122).[30] It is a small church, 18 m in length and 8 m in width, with a single nave of two bays that end in a polygonal choir (FIG. 36c). To the north of the apse a two-story building is attached: a sacristy with an upper story. There is no information about the upper story, and its purpose is difficult to guess. It probably had a wooden floor.

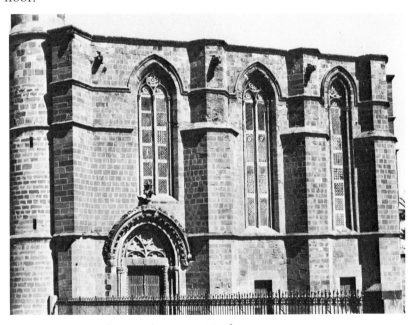

Plate 122. Saint Catherine of Nicosia. Northern side.

On the southern side of the apse rose a small tower with a spiral staircase that the Turks transformed into a minaret. Previously it had led to the terrace of the church. In the interior Saint Catherine is vaulted with rib vaults. The ribs rest on clusters of three columns engaged in the wall, similar to those at Saint George of the Latins. They also resemble those of the refectory of Bella Pais. On the outside, the wall is reinforced by octagonal buttresses. Between these buttresses the windows create long, narrow bands that end in pointed arches, as at Saint George of the Latins. They have embrasures only on the outside. A thin mullion divides two small arcades, at the top of which is a tracery with a trefoil. The window that opens onto the room north of the choir is smaller and corresponds to the upper floor.

The elevation is divided in two by a band with a dripstone profile that underlines the base of the windows. On each side of the first bay are doors with round arches and molded voussoirs. The jambs are ornamented with colonnettes just like the windows. The tympana of the southern and western portals have traceries formed by two blind arches and a blind quatrefoil. The archivolts are enriched by lacy foliage treated very naturalistically.

The western portal has a marble lintel decorated by four dragons that divide two roses. The northern door is more damaged, but one can distinguish on it the same decorations as on the other two. The corbels that carry the archivolts are sculpted with fantastic animal and human forms.

Among others, one of the corbels under the tracery of the portal is decorated by a double rose, another by a head with curly hair. This door led to another building whose use is not known. The choir has a niche on the southern side ornamented with a gable very richly decorated with patterns of small flowers.

On the upper part of the buttresses a small drain gathers the rainwater and lets it run toward the gargoyle. The rich foliage of all these churches in Cyprus has no parallel in Greece except in the southern chapel of Saint Paraskevi at Chalkis.

Since World War II the churches of Saint George of the Latins and Saint Catherine, as well as the whole town of Famagusta, are in the Turkish area of Cyprus and at present there is little interest in their preservation or restoration.

Conclusion

The churches discussed in this book are primarily Latin monastic churches. They were completely built by the Franks, except for Daphni and Vlachernes, earlier churches to which they made certain additions. The Byzantine influence on these churches manifested only on rare occasions such as at Vlachernes or Saint Nicolas of Isova, where Greek workers were employed. Certainly these were not the only churches in Greece built by the Franks, but the others are completely ruined and can only be named, not described. In Cyprus there are, of course, also the cathedrals of Nicosia and Famagusta, but these have no relationship to the monastic churches of the mendicant orders and are closer in spirit to the thirteenth- and fourteenth-century cathedrals of the West.

The Frankish churches of Greece all present a rectangular plan without a projecting transept (except perhaps for Saint Peter Martyr of Candia, which in its original form probably did have one), a rectangular or polygonal apse, and usually a double-pitched wooden roof. Only their apses are vaulted, except for Saint Mark of Candia. The masonry is almost always of ashlar, and bricks are used only to fill in holes. The two-story elevation becomes more popular in the thirteenth century and continues to be used in the fourteenth century in both modest and richer buildings all over Europe. Flying buttresses are less necessary for the more modest height of these buildings, and vertical buttresses replace them.

The sculptured decoration is not very rich, since it was not encouraged by the monastic orders for whom the churches were built. The preference was for foliated motifs, and one can find hardly any representations of the human form.

The greatest influence came from Burgundy in the thirteenth century and also from the south of France and Italy. In Crete, Italy plays the most important role; in Cyprus, the art of Champagne and Catalonia have had the greatest influence.

Romanesque features often persist within Italian Gothic architecture and are also apparent in buildings constructed outside Italy. The solid massive walls are not a deviation from the Gothic style of these buildings but an integral part of it.

Around the entire Mediterranean Sea, except Cyprus, the flat mural effect in its simplest, most solid and rectangular form continued to develop in the interior and exterior of structures. The area reserved for windows was never very large except in the sanctuary, which usually tried to focus attention by greater luminosity. The sculptured decor of the capitals and the vaults creates an agreeable contrast and again draws attention.

The spacious Latin churches do not create a metaphysical or transcendental atmosphere but reaffirm the same logic as the Cistercian churches.

Western influence on Byzantine architecture was never extensive, and one is surprised to find the rare examples of it. The most important reason for this lack of exchange of forms is that relations between the Greeks and the Latins always remained distant. The difference between the Roman Catholic rites and the Greek Orthodox rites also encouraged the difference in architectural forms. As long as the Franks were conquerors, they had very little influence on the Greeks.

Paradoxically, it is during the period before the Fourth Crusade that one finds an exchange of forms between Byzantium and the West.[1] Not only did Byzantium influence Western art, but as early as the twelfth century it encouraged commercial contact with the West. It is then that we find in Greece forms that could only be due to these trade relations. The church of Palaiopanagia (Monolada) and the church of the Dormition of the Virgin at Merbeka[2] are good examples. Much later, in the seventeenth and eighteenth centuries, one finds examples like the church of Hypapanti in Athens or the interiors of notable villas (*archontika*), primarily in northern and central Greece, decorated according to Western taste and style.

The limited Western influence one finds in Greece in the Middle Ages during the Latin occupation appears in the vaulted areas of Byzantine churches; in the decorations of doors and windows; and in the elongated plans, which become more common.

There has recently been discovered at "Osios Loukas," under a tower of the Byzantine monastery, a small chapel whose ribbed

Plate 123. Osios Loukas. Vault of the chapel.

vault, made of bricks, belongs to the eleventh century (PLATE 123). Its construction is entirely different from that of Western vaults, being formed by a row of bricks parallel to each other and protruding approximately seven inches from the vault, but its existence warrants notice.[3]

Also in the neighborhood of Athens, a small church belonging to the second half of the twelfth century,[4] known as "Omorphe Ecclesia," has ribbed vaults in its small southern chapel.[5] Another, called Saint John Magouti of Athens, a Byzantine church with ribbed vaults, is now completely destroyed.[6] Other examples of stylistic interpenetration are the church of Saint Athanassios of Chalandritsa of the fifteenth century, a Byzantine church built after the Frankish occupation,[7] and the monastery of Daou Pentelis, whose narthex, covered by ribbed vaults, dates from the sixteenth century. The windows, niches, and portals with pointed arches decorated with moldings or traceries of trefoils and roses generally show Western influence on Byzantine architecture. The pointed arch by itself can be misleading, for it was also used by the Turks and continues to appear in Greece until the eighteenth century. For this reason the cloister of Daphni was long believed to be a Western structure, whereas today we know it belongs to the period after the Cistercian monks had left Greece. At Gastouni, Saint Mary Catholikos, a Byzantine church of the twelfth century, has a door on the northern side, later blocked off, where one can discern a pointed arch formed by four blocks whose extrados is underlined by a row of bricks and whose voussoir is carved with a chamfer molding that forms five teeth on each side. The colonnettes in the exterior angles have decorated capitals with foliage that can only be of the thirteenth century.[8]

In Androusa the Byzantine church of Saint George has a small northern door with a pointed arch whose ring moldings, along with the archivolt with protruding stones and a beveled fillet, give the impression of having been executed at the beginning of the thirteenth century by Greek workers who knew certain Western methods of construction.[9]

At Geraki in Morea, one finds several churches with pointed arches around the doorways and niches.[10] They are situated either in the village under the fortress or in the palace itself. The most important sculptured sections are the *proskynitari* of Saint Paraskevi, the door of the "Zoodochos Pege," (PLATE 124), the doors and a niche of the chapel no. 4[11] in the village, and the door of the narthex as well as the *proskynitari* of the church of Saint George

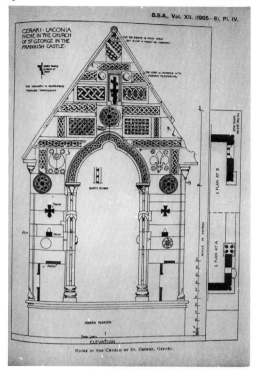

Plate 124. *Saint George of Geraki "proskynitari,"*
1230–75.

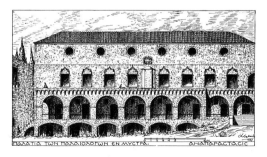

Fig. 37. *Mistras. Palace of the Paleologos.*

in the castle of Geraki. Bon has described them in great detail.[12] None of the details of decoration of the niches or portals can be directly related to those we have come across in this study, but they are of interest because they must have been done while Geraki was the seat of the barony of the Nivelets, whose coat of arms can be seen in many parts of the castle; that is, they were executed during the period of 1230 to 1275 by Greek workers for their Frankish masters.

The style of the *proskynitari* of the church of Saint George in the castle of Geraki is a combination of more than one style. Certain details are Western, others are Saracen or Mohammedan and could have been brought back from the Holy Land, and others are naturally Byzantine. One could say this sculptural decoration constitutes a new style formed by the fusion of more than one element; this was perpetuated at Mistra in the Peloponnesus in the fifteenth century and even into the seventeenth century. A good example, which Orlandos studies, is afforded by the framing in porous stone of the windows of the palace of Mistra (FIG. 37), of the period between 1250 and 1350.[13] Similarly, one can observe the influence of Gothic architecture in the fifteenth-century bell tower of Pantanassa at Mistra (PLATE 125). This has often been pointed out. Enlart saw in it the influence of Champagne and the Gothic style of the thirteenth century.[14] But here too we discern a combination of motifs, and it reminds one more strongly of the cathedral of Palermo. It was built too late to have been directly influenced by the Frankish monuments built in Greece after the Fourth Crusade.

Crete has several examples of Western portals spread out over the whole island.[15]

Very interesting are the ruins of the Byzantine church of the Holy Apostles in the region of Sykaminos of Oropos in Attica. On the northern side near the sanctuary, a pointed arch was found whose moldings are in a Western style.[16] The same place yielded capitals executed for the Venetians, for one of them carries the coat of arms of the Venetian family of Foscarini. They must date from the end of the thirteenth century or the beginning of the fourteenth.

The church of the Parigoritissa of Arta, a Byzantine church built between 1389 and 1396 by Michael II of Epirus, is also extremely impressive. The most extraordinary feature is the interior part under the dome, which rests on four rows of superimposed columns crowned by pointed arches and ornamented with sculptural reliefs (FIG. 38). Most of the capitals of the columns are early Christian and were taken from ancient monuments.[17] By contrast, the columns in the third row are in a Western style; they stand in pairs at the angle of the wall. These columns have sculptured bases that represent monsters and remind one vividly of the Romanesque style (FIG. 39). They seem to represent animals from the Apocalypse or the symbols of the Evangelists. Their capitals are not Byzantine either. Their stylized leaves must have been modeled on Western capitals of the beginning of the twelfth century. Sculptured arches, also sculpted in high relief, rest on colonnettes under the dome. The placement of the figures reminds one of the portals of Romanesque and Gothic churches.

Plate 125. Pantanassa, Mistra. Fifteenth century. The apse and bell tower.

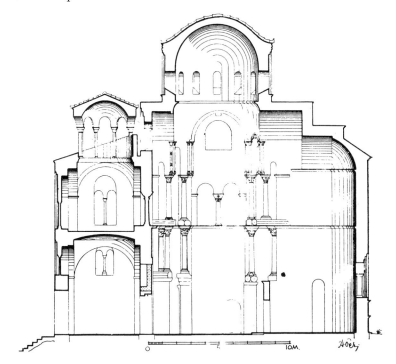

Fig. 38. Parigoritissa of Arta. Longitudinal cut. Drawing by Orlandos.

A sculptural program of such dimensions could not, of course, be Byzantine. According to Orlandos, Italian artists had been brought in by the Despot of Epirus, whose relations with the Italian families of Orsini in Cephalonia and the Angevins of Naples were very close.

Except in the case of the Parigoritissa of Arta, one cannot speak with certainty of the influence of a single country or region on the

Byzantine architecture or decorative sculptural elements in Greece, any more than one can relate the Western buildings in Greece to a single region of France, Italy, or Spain, such as Burgundy, Champagne, or Catalonia.

Fig. 39. Parigoritissa of Arta: capitals and bases of columns.

One often forgets that in the Middle Ages artisans traveled far from their native soil. In addition, the monastic orders became an

Conclusion

international force after the thirteenth century and spread over all of Europe without regard to nationality.

The forms found in Greece are for this reason disparate; they correspond to the spirit of various monastic orders whose purpose was primarily missionary rather than the glorification of God through art. These orders were accustomed to an architecture that one finds mostly in Burgundy and the Mediterranean regions of southern France, Catalonia, Italy, and Greece. Of the twenty churches studied—certainly not the only ones that existed in Greece and Cyprus—all were built by Westerners. They are purely Western works, on Western models, hardly ever with any noticeable Byzantine influence (FIGS. 35, 36) except perhaps in isolated instances, such as in Arta or perhaps in the mural paintings of the Cretan churches that have disappeared. All the churches have elongated rectangular plans, flat or polygonal eastern choirs, and pointed wooden tie-beam roofs. Most often only the choir is covered by a ribbed vault. They often have a two-story elevation, a form that becomes more noticeable in the West in the second half of the thirteenth century and which in Venice has parallels in the churches of Giovanni Paolo, Santa Maria dei Frari, and San Nicolo at Treviso. It eliminates the flying buttress and substitutes the vertical flat buttress. The sculptural decor is not very rich, since this was hardly encouraged by the Cistercians and mendicant orders. The influence of this style on Byzantine architecture was almost nil, mostly because during the whole Latin occupation the Greeks felt extremely antagonistic toward their Catholic rulers. On the mainland of Greece some Western characteristics are noticeable but have sometimes been overlooked, for their characteristics are often too simple. In the Greek churches built after the beginning of the thirteenth century, one can often notice a lengthening of the plan, colonnettes at the angles, and running half-barrel vaults. These were certainly in their origin characteristic of Western architecture and were to a great extent dispersed by the monastic orders. But more important for Gothic art, they represent a remarkable expansion, with Western forms spread across all of Europe and the Mediterranean to the Greek mainland, Crete, and Cyprus.

Notes

Preface

1. A. Bon, *LaMorée Franque: Recherches historiques, topographiques et archéologiques sur la principauté d'Achaie (1205–1430)* (Paris, 1969).
2. G. Gerola, *I Monumenti Veneti nell' Isola di Creta* (Venice, 1908–38).
3. C. Enlart, *L'art gothique et la Renaissance en Chypre* (Paris, 1899). Also, R. B. Francis, *The Medieval Churches of Cyprus* (London, 1949).
4. The word "Franks" is used here with the Greek meaning *fragoi*, employed for the Roman Catholic Crusaders in general regardless of their origin. The word "Latins" is used in the same sense, not necessarily limited to Mediterraneans. It is the equivalent of "Westerners." The Venetians are always mentioned separately by the Greeks because they acted independently of the other Crusaders and remained in Greece much longer.

Chapter One

1. J. Longnon, *L'empire latin de Constantinople et la principauté de Morée,* (Paris, 1949), p. 15, mentions that Venice was given the first privilege in Constantinople in 1082 because it had helped Alexis Comnenos against the Normans. R. Janin, *La géographie écclésiastique de l'empire byzantin* (Paris, 1953), 3:582; Charles Diehl, *La république de Venise* (Paris, 1967), p. 66. Heinrich Kretschmayer, *Geschichte von Venedig* (Gotha, 1905–20), 1:161.
2. It is not yet clear if Venice was the only or most important factor in the rerouting of the Fourth Crusade. M. Luchaire, *Innocent III et la question de l'Orient* (Paris, 1907), finds it impossible to answer this question from the data at our disposal. Also Fr. Thiriet, *La Romanie vénitienne au moyen âge* (Paris, 1959), p. 65, believes that the great historian C. Hopf (1832–73), exaggerated the responsibility of Venice. Diehl, *La république de Venise,* p. 68.
3. The most important are G. Villehardouin, *De la conquête de Constantinople par les barons français associés aux Vénitiens l'an 1204,* ed. E. Faral (Paris, 1938–39); Henri de Valenciennes, "L'histoire de l'empereur Henri de Constantinople," in *Documents relatifs à l'histoire des croisades,* ed. J. Longnon (Paris, 1948); and Robert de Clari, *La conquête de Constantinople,* in Les classiques français du moyen âge, ed. Ph. Lauer, vol. 40 (Paris, 1924).
4. Villehardouin, *Conquête de Constantinople,* 1:97.

5. Ibid., p. 203.

6. Particularly, Nicea in Bithynia on the Asiatic side of the Sea of Marmara grew into a strong power, from which the Greeks began to challenge the Franks. On 25 July 1261, Greek forces from Nicea recaptured Constantinople in a completely unexpected move and drove the Latin emperor Baudouin II into exile.

7. J. Longnon, "Problèmes de l'histoire de la principauté de Morée," *Journal des Savants* (1946), pp. 178–85, says it was probably the territory between Mesynopolis and Salonika and also Boeotia, Corinth, and the Argolis.

8. Longnon, *Empire latin*, p. 60.

9. Stephanos Xanthoudides, *He Enetokratia en Krete kai oi Kata ton Eneton Agones ton Kreton* [The Venetian occupation of Crete and the struggle of the Cretans against Venice]. *Byzantinische Neugriechische Jahrbücher*, no. 39 (Athens, 1939), p. 4. Also Kretschmayer, *Geschichte von Venedig*, 1:317.

10. William Miller, *Essays on the Latin Orient* (Amsterdam, 1964), p. 61.

11. The history of the kingdom of Cyprus is independent of the historical development of the empire of Constantinople. It was in the hands of the Franks as early as 1191. The island of Rhodes, on the contrary, was conquered much later, in 1309, by the Hospitalers of Saint John. At the time Constantinople surrendered, Rhodes was in the hands of the very powerful Greek Leon Gavalas, and the terms of the 1204 partition ceding it to the Venetians were never fulfilled.

12. Giulio Bistori, *La Repubblica di Venezia delle trasmigrazioni nelle laguna fino alle caduta di Constantinopoli 1453* (Venice, 1916), p. 150. Roberto Cessi, *Storia della Repubblica di Venezia* (Milan, 1944), 1:189–93. Diehl, *République de Venise*, p. 69.

13. Luchaire, *Innocent III*, pp. 85, 91, 97.

14. A. Potthast, *Regesta pontificum Romanorum inde ab anno post Christum natum 1198 ad 1304* (Berlin, 1874–75), p. 335, 29 July 1198: pl. 214, pp. 334–36 (ep. j. 358).

15. Elizabeth A. R. Brown, "The Cistercians in the Latin Empire of Constantinople and Greece," *Traditio* 14(1958):68.

16. Villehardouin, *Conquête de Constantinople*, 1:46–47.

17. Potthast, *Regesta pontificum Romanorum*, p. 559, 5 January 1199: pl. 214, pp. 470–71 (ep. i. 508).

18. J. N. Canivez, "Citeaux (Orde)," In *Dictionnaire d'histoire et de géographie écclesiastique*, pp. 898–902, mentions that the Cistercians had taken part in the Crusades as early as the twelfth century.

19. Brown, "Cistercians in the Latin Empire," pp. 77–78.

20. Angel Manrique, *Cistercienses seu verius ecclesiastici annales a condito Cistercio* (Lyons, 1642–59)3:435.

21. Brown, "Cistercians in the Latin Empire," p. 78.

22. Ibid., p. 81.

23. G. Millet, *Le monastère de Daphni* (Paris, 1899), pp. 57–58; Longnon, *L'empire latin*, pp. 118–19.

24. Brown, "Cistercians in the Latin Empire"; F. Gregorovius, *Geschichte der Stadt Athen im Mittelalter* (Stuttgart, 1889), 1:340; Millet, *Daphni*, p. 28; J. Gautier, *Othon de la Roche conquérant d'Athènes et sa famille*,

Matériaux archéologiques inédits (Besançon: Academie des Sciences, Belles-Lettres et Arts de Besançon, 1880), p. 143.

25. In 1217, Gervase, patriarch of Constantinople, asked the general chapter of the Cistercians to incorporate the monastery of the Mount Sancti Gregorii, which could have been confused with the name Gergeri. This idea was proposed by Brown, "Cistercians in the Latin Empire," p. 85, but there is no indication in the *Statutes* of the place where the monastery was situated.

26. Flaminio Cornaro (Flaminius Cornelius), *Creta Sacra* (Venice, 1755), pp. 20–21, 35.

27. J. M. Canivez, *Statua selecta capitulorum generalium ordinis Cisterciensis ab anno 1116 ad annum 1786* (Louvain, 1933–41), 3:122–23, no. 40.

28. Brown, "Cistercians in the Latin Empire," p. 83.

29. Ibid.

30. R. Clair, "Les filles de Hautecombe dans l'empire latin de Constantinople," *Analecta Sacri Ordinis Cisterciensis* 17(1961):262–68.

31. Canivez, *Statua,* 2:47, no. 59.

32. Ibid., 2:232, no. 15. The name here is Saracaz and not Zaraka, as it is known today.

33. L. Wadding, *Annales minorum seu trium ordinum* (Rome, 1731–1886), 2:286.

34. Ibid., 1:303, 4:133.

35. Millet, *Daphni,* pp. 36–37.

36. Raymond Loenertz, "Documents pour servir à l'histoire de la province dominicaine de Grèce, 1474–1660," *Archivum Fratrum Praedicatorum* 14(1944):74. This is a call addressed to the brothers of the order by the master Humbert Romans in 1235.

37. Cornaro, *Creta Sacra,* 1:220–28. In the absence of documents from the Dominican province, one is obliged to look for its history in the writings of scholars of the order, of the church, and in secular authorities. The general chapters of the order are of greatest value during the thirteenth to fifteenth centuries. After 1474 the registers of the general masters become more informative.

38. Loenertz, "Documents," 14:76. His opinion is that the document must be in error here, for it makes Saint Peter's monastery appear at least a century and a half younger. In this document the author attributes the foundation of the monastery to the Dominican father Saint Vincent Ferrer. He could, however, have known the history of James of Milan from Dominican writers, for his tomb was venerated in the church of the monastery of Saint Peter's in the thirteenth century.

39. Also mentioned by Flaminio Cornaro, *Creta Sacra*, vol. 2.

40. Ibid., 2:29. Also, Giuseppe Gerola, *I Monumenti Veneti nell' Isola di Creta* (Venice, 1908–38), 3:141, 4:344.

41. Ibid., 3:144–45.

42. Luchaire, *Innocent III,* pp. 165–66.

43. Ibid., pp. 153, 159.

44. Ibid., p. 186.

45. Loenertz, "Documents," 14:76.

46. Bon, *Morée Franque,* p. 97. P. Pressuti, *Regestum Honorii III* (Rome, 1885–95), 2:50, no. 3844. The list of the episcopal sees was given in the

agreement of 1223 of Giovanni Colonna, cardinal of Saint Pressede, who in 1217 had received from the pope the power to unite and divide the churches, pl. 216, col. 969.

47. Loenertz, "Marino Dandolo et son conflit avec l'évêque Jean," *Orientalia Christiana Periodica*, 25(1959):169.

48. Innocent III, *Epistolae 13* (153), pl. 216, col. 331. This letter is addressed to the bishop of Davlia (Davatiensi et Zoratoriensi episcopis).

49. Thiriet, *Romanie vénitienne*, pp. 98–99.

50. Bon, *Morée Franque*, pp. 98–99.

51. Thiriet, *Romanie vénitienne*, p. 125.

52. N. Papadakis, He *Ekklesia Kretes: Episkopai, Monai* (Canea, Crete, 1936), p. 30.

53. Ibid.; this date is not certain.

54. Thiriet, *Romanie vénitienne*; see map, p. 83.

55. For a detailed bibliography on Frankish Greece (to about 1962), see pp. 908–38 in *The Cambridge Medieval History*, 4, part 1 (Cambridge University Press, 1966).

Chapter Two

1. According to Villehardouin, *Conquête de Constantinople*, 2:111 (302–5), end of September 1204.

2. In Greece no land had been kept for the emperor.

3. Villehardouin, *Conquête de Constantinople*, 2:139.

4. Ibid., 2:141–43.

5. Bon, *Morée Franque*, pp. 75–76.

6. Ibid.

7. Ibid., pp. 151–52.

8. Kenneth Setton, *Catalan Domination of Athens, 1311–1388* (Cambridge, Mass., 1948), pp. 125–48.

9. The term "Romania" was used even before the Fourth Crusade. It applied to the lands under the domination of the emperor of the Romans. The eastern Roman Empire with its new capital established by Constantine became Romania. This is also the opinion of F. Thiriet, *Romanie vénitienne*, map, p. 83, in contrast to R. L. Wolff, "Romania: The Latin Empire of Constantinople," *Speculum* 23 (1948):1–34.

10. Bon, *Morée Franque*, p. 66.

11. Thiriet, *Romanie vénitienne*, map, p. 185; the protectorate of the Aegean incorporated the duchy of Naxos or of the Archipelagos, pp. 245–51.

12. This is the most difficult to evaluate from the documents.

13. Thiriet, *Romanie vénitienne*, pp. 126–28.

14. Ibid., p. 93. Also Kretschmayer, *Geschichte von Venedig*, 2:23.

15. Thiriet, *Romanie vénitienne*, p. 59.

16. Jean Longnon, *Les français d'outre-mer au moyen-âge* (Paris, 1929).

17. Kretschmayer, *Geschichte von Venedig*, 2:388–92.

Chapter Three

1. Brown, *Cistercians in the Latin Empire*, p. 72. Millet, *Daphni*, p. 25.

2. Saracaz is a latinization of the word Zaraka, the name of the Greek valley where this monastery was built. The Cistercians habitually named their monasteries for the area; for instance, at Clara Vallis the monastery

was Clairvaux, at Hauterive, Altariva, Beau-mont, and so forth. What is strange here is that they did not prefer a French name to a Greek one.

3. Robert Branner, *Burgundian Gothic Architecture* (London, 1960), p. 13; Marcel Aubert, "Existe-t-il une architecture cistercienne?" *Cahiers de Civilisation Mediévale* 1(1958):153–58; F. Bucher, *Zisterzienserabtei: Notre Dame de Bonmont* (Bern, 1957), p. 47.

4. Branner, *Burgundian Gothic*, p. 13.

5. Anselme Dimier, *Les moines bâtisseurs* (Paris, 1964), p. 101.

6. As, for example, the demand of G. Villehardouin to the general chapter in 1225.

7. H. Sejalon, "Institutions du chapitre géneral cistercien, *Monasticon cisterciense*," ed. E. Solesmes (Rome, 1892), p. 212. This is inspired by a Benedictine rule demanding that the monks divorce themselves from everyday life. Bucher, *Notre Dame de Bonmont*, p. 47.

8. "Semper enim valles, silvestris undique cinctas, arboribus divus Vernardus amoenaque prata et fluvius," Bruchius, *Monasterium Germaniae*, 1:103. In Bucher, *Notre Dame de Bonmont*, p. 47.

9. E. Viollet-le-Duc, *Dictionnaire raisonné d'architecture française* (Paris, 1854), 1:313–14, says this plan originated with the Roman town, was continued in the Merovingian period, then was used in the monastery of Saint Gall and at Cluny.

10. Marcel Aubert, *Architecture cistercienne en France* (Paris, 1943), p. 208.

11. It is not known to whom the church was dedicated. Generally Cistercian churches were consecrated to the Virgin.

12. Canivez, *Statuta*, vol. 2, no. 35 (1241), no. 39 (1257), pp. 232, 432; Lucien Auvray, *Les registres de Gregoire IX* (Paris, 1907), vol. 9, no. 3878; A. Orlandos, *Mélanges offerts à Octave et Melpo Merlier* (Athens, 1955); Bon, *Morée Franque*, p. 553, places it at the beginning of the thirteenth century; Millet, *Daphni*, p. 311, gives the date as 1223–24.

13. Clair, "Filles de Hautecombe," pp. 262–66, suggests that the abbey of Zaraka was established by the monks of Hautecombe, who had been asked to do so in 1210. Often the dates of the founding of a monastery and of the construction of its buildings are not the same, for the monks were not usually rich enough to build their abbey immediately after the land was donated.

14. Clair, "Filles de Hautecombe," p. 263, also Innocent III, *Epistolae 13* (168); Brown, "Cistercians in the Latin Empire," p. 87, says this foundation was established in Patras perhaps before 1212. There could be some confusion here, for in 1210 Anselme offered to Cluny the monastery of Hierokomio near Patras (see Clair, "Les filles de Hautecombe," p. 263). Also the order of Saint Ruf was called by the archbishop in 1210 (see Innocent III, *Epistolae 13* (159–60).

15. Canivez, *Statuta*, vol. 2, no. 59, p. 47.

16. Bon, *Morée Franque*, p. 100.

17. A Rangaves, *Excursion en Arcadie*, pp. 402–3, mentioned by Bon, *Morée Franque*, pp. 553–54.

18. Bucher, *Notre Dame de Bonmont*, p. 184, where he makes a classification of the Cistercian plans.

19. Aubert, *Architecture cistercienne*, p. 211.

20. Orlandos, *Mélanges*, p. 14.

21. "Turres lapideae ad campanas non fiant." Canivez, *Statuta*, ann. 1157.

22. Aubert, *Architecture cistercienne*, p. 142.

23. J. Bilson, "The Architecture of the Cistercians," *Archaeological Journal* (London, 1909), p. 228.

24. Bon, *Morée Franque*, p. 557.

25. Orlandos, *Mélanges*, p. 14.

26. Henri Focillon, *The Art of the West* (London, 1963), 2:48.

27. Aubert, *Architecture cistercienne*, p. 24, fig. 18.

28. Bilson, "Architecture of the Cistercians," p. 197.

29. C. Enlart, *Origines françaises de l'architecture gothique en Italie* (Paris, 1894), p. 291.

30. Bon, *Morée Franque*, p. 557.

31. Ibid., p. 557, pl. 120 d–g.

32. Orlandos, *Mélanges*, p. 8.

33. Only parts of the ruined walls are still standing, some up to 7 m high.

34. L. Janauschek, *Originum Cisterciensium* (Venice, 1877), vol. 2. In his genealogical chart he shows that the church of Fossanova was a filial of the monastery of Hautecombe of the diocese of Geneva. According to Clair, "Filles de Hautecombe," Zaraka may have been built by the monks of Hautecombe, with whom Innocent III had come in contact in 1210 at the request of the archbishop. But they could have also have come from Fossanova.

35. R. Branner, "Paris and the Origins of Rayonnant Gothic Architecture down to 1240," *Art Bulletin* 48 (March 1962):39, fig. 1.

36. Janauschek, *Originum*, 1 (no. 588):227 had placed the founding of the monastery of Zaraka in 1224.

37. W. M. Leake, *Travels in the Morea* (London, 1830), 2:87–89.

38. J. A. C. Buchon, *La Grèce continentale et la Morée: Voyage, séjour et études historiques en 1840, 1841, 1843* (Paris, 1843), pp. 497–98.

39. J. A. C. Buchon, *Atlas des nouvelles recherches historiques sur la principauté française de Morée* (Paris, 1845), pl. 31. Fr. Lenormant, "Le monastère de Daphni près d'Athènes sous la domination des Princes croisés," in *Revue archéologique* (Paris, 1872), pls. 3 and 4. He believed that the porch of Daphni was Benedictine.

40. N. Moutsopoulos, "Le monastère franc de Notre Dame d'Isova, Gortynie," *Bulletin de Correspondance Héllenique* 80(1956):77–78; also his article "Frangikes Ekklesies sten Hellada," *Technika Chronika* 1(1960):7. Also R. Traquair, "Frankish Architecture in Greece," *Journal of the Royal Institute of British Architects*, 3d ser., 31 (nos. 2 and 3):2 (reprint).

41. *Chronikon tou Moreos*, ed. J. Schmitt (London, 1904), reproduced by P. Kolonaros, (Athens, 1940), p. 197, lines 4671–72; "Sten Isovan ethiaveken allagi apo tous Tourkous, to monasteri ekapsasi ethe amartia pou eginei." Also D. Zakynthinos, *Le despotat grec de Morée* (Paris, 1932), 1:35, 37. *Chronicle of Morea* French version, p. 201, lines 4793–95, also gives us the name, but we have no information on the foundation of the church. Its name is even today surrounded by legends, and the peasants of the area speak of this monastery as *ta palatia*, "palaces." Perhaps its existence was of very short duration, for no document mentions it.

42. Traquair, "Frankish Architecture," p. 7.

43. Ibid., p. 6, fig. 5; Bon, *Morée Franque*, pl. 62B.

44. Buchon, *Grèce continentale*, pp. 497–98.

45. Bon, *Morée Franque*, p. 539, also accepts the existence on this side of a door that communicated with the lower level of the cloister.

46. Traquair, "Frankish Architecture," p. 4, fig. 5; also Bon, *Morée franque*, p. 542.

47. Bon, *Morée Franque*, p. 538.

48. Viollet-le-Duc, *Dictionnaire raisonné*, 2:87.

49. Bon, *Morée Franque*, p. 540, fig. 2B, and p. 542.

50. Ibid., p. 539.

51.. Traquair, "Frankish Architecture," pp. 1, 5, fig. 6, has made a reconstruction of the church and the monastic buildings; also Bon, *Morée Franque*, pl. 57.

52. P. Lavedan, *L'architecture gothique religieuse en Catalogne, Valence et Baleares* (Paris, 1935), p. 16.

53. Clair, "Filles de Hautecombe," p. 266; also see Bon, *Morée Franque*, p. 101. The church of Corinth, from which the monastery of Zaraka depended, was reconstructed only after 1212. Until the archbishop of Patras was in charge of the whole region.

54. Brown, "Cistercians in the Latin Empire," p. 87; Clair, "Filles de Hautecombe," p. 263; Innocent III, *Epistolae 13*, November 1210 (168), cols. 341–42, in *Patrologie latine de Migne*, p. 216 (Paris, 1855).

55. Canivez, *Statuta* (1225), pp. 47, 59. "Petitio principis achaiae de construendo monasterio ordinia nostri committitur abbati Morimundi." Bon, *Morée Franque*, p. 100, says that the Cistercians established themselves also at Andravida. Clair, "Filles de Hautecombe," p. 266; Brown, "Cistercians in the Latin Empire," p. 87.

56. A. Dimier, *Recueil de plans d'églises cisterciennes* (Paris, 1949), pls. 25, 33, 43, 55, 78. 133.

57. A. De Dion, "Notes sur l'architecture de l'ordre de Grandmont," *Bulletin Monumental* (1874). The church at Belmont has been considered by certain authors to resemble the plans of the churches of Grandmont.

58. Aubert, "Existe-t-il une architecture cistercienne?" p. 156.

59. Brown, "Cistercians in the Latin Empire," p. 87.

60. Lavedan, *Architecture gothique*, p. 14.

61. R. P. Meerseman, "L'architecture dominicaine du 13e siècle: Législation et pratique," *Archivum Fratum Praedicatorum* 16 (1946):147. The Dominicans, Franciscans, and Cistercians were forbidden to use stone vaults over their naves, since this was less expensive and appeared more modest. But the rule was not always followed.

62. Jacques Thirion, *L'ancienne église de Lamourguier* (Le Roussillon, 1954), pp. 432–45.

63. Marcel Durliat, *L'art dans de royaume de Majorque* (Paris, 1962), pp. 72–73.

64. Enlart, *Origines françaises*, pp. 102–7.

65. Traquair, "Frankish Architecture," also mentions the similarity between the church of Isova and the dormitory of Fossanova, but without suggesting a direct influence. He mentions a greater similarity between the Hotel-Dieu of Tonnerre in Burgundy and Our Lady. This building, which ends to the east in a polygonal apse, dates from 1293–1308—too late for Isova. For the plan, see Viollet-le-Duc, *Dictionnaire raisonné*, 6:108, fig.

6. Moutsopoulos, "Monastère franc," p. 90, speaks of the wooden peaked roofs of the cathedral of Ely and the great hall of Westminster Abbey, both of the fourteenth century and certainly with no relationship of either style or origin to the church of Isova.

66. Viollet-le-Duc, *Dictionnaire raisonné*, 1:5, says polygonal apses were preferred in Provence. The cathedral of Toulouse offers a good example of a single nave as found in southern French architecture at the beginning of the thirteenth century.

67. Dimier, *Moines bâtisseurs*, p. 110. The influence of Fossanova is also found in many of the daughter houses of Morimond, even outside Italy.

68. For the other orders established in Morea, see Bon, *Morée Franque*, pp. 100–102.

69. Traquair, "Frankish Architecture," p. 9, fig. 10. He made very exact representations of them. Also see Enlart, *Origines*, pp. 279–80.

70. Traquair, "Frankish Architecture," p. 8, fig. 9.

71. Moutsopoulos, "Frangikes Ekklesies sten Hellada," p. 10, fig. 8, believes it is another door that was later eliminated and does not indicate it on his reconstruction.

72. Bon, *Morée Franque*, pl. 65.

73. Traquair, "Frankish Architecture," fig. 10.

74. Other parts were found in the ruins, as for instance a fragment of a trefoiled arcade, today incorporated in a fountain not far from Saint Nicolas. Also a round marble basin 1.58 m in diameter that must have been used to collect water from neighboring sources. Bon, *Morée Franque*, p. 546, pls. 62c and d, fig. 4.

75. Moutsopoulos, "Monastère franc," p. 80.

76. Traquair, "Frankish Architecture," p. 10.

77. Bon, *Morée Franque*, p. 547.

78. In southern Italy, Gothic architecture was introduced in 1266 by Charles I of Anjou, king of Naples, who had brought with him French workmen. These Angevin rulers of Naples governed Morea in the fourteenth century. For several centuries in the past, the south of Italy had also been in contact with Byzantine art.

79. F. C. H. Pouqueville, *Voyage de la Grèce*, 2d ed. (Paris, 1827), 5.135.

80. Millet, *Daphni*, p. 3.

81. G. A. Soteriou, *Christianike kai Vyzantine Archaiologia* (Athens, 1942), 1:427. Millet, *Daphni*, says the refectory and the chapel of the cemetery are of the same period.

82. E. Stikas, "Stereosis kai Apokatastasis tou Exonarthekos tou Katholikou tes Mones Dafniou," *Deltion Christianikes Archaiologikes Hetaireias*, extracts of (Athens, 1962), ser. 4, pp. 1–49.

83. Millet, *Daphni*, p. 31.

84. Gregorovius, *Geschichte der Stadt Athen*, 1:340. Also Gauthier, *Othon de la Roche*, p. 143. By the same author, *Les inscriptions des abbayes cisterciennes du Diocèse de Besançon*, Besançon, 1882, pp. 299–336.

85. Millet, *Daphni*, p. 1, says that the pilgrims from the West did not come through Daphni on their way to the Holy Land. They crossed over to Corfu, Lepanto, Thessaly, or Messinia and the Aegean Sea.

86. It is also known as Dalphini until 1458; Millet, *Daphni*, p. 25. Buchon had seen laurels that do not exist today, Buchon, *Grèce continentale*, p. 173.

87. Stikas, "Stereosis," ser. 4, pp. 1–49.

88. Buchon, *Atlas*, pl. 31; Lenormant, "Daphni," p. 282; Millet, *Daphni*, p. 57, pl. 2.

89. A. Orlandos, "Neotera Evremata eis ten Monen Dafniou," *Archeion Vyzantinon Mnemeion tes Hellados* 8 (1955–56):69. In the seventeenth century there were only two Greek monks, according to Spon and Wheeler, who visited it in 1679. Spon and Wheeler, *Voyage d'Italie, de Dalmatie, de Gréce . . . 1678–79* (Amsterdam, 1679), 2:275.

90. Millet, *Daphni*, p. 25.

91. C. Enlart, "Quelques monuments d'architecture gothique en Grèce," *Revue de l'Art Chrétien*, 4th ser., 8(1897):309, thought the porch was early eighteenth century. Today this date does not seem to fit the style of its arcades.

92. Millet, *Daphni*, p. 57; Stikas, "Stereosis," p. 21.

93. Lenormant, "Daphni," pp. 232, 245, 279–89, considers the portal to have been built by the Latins. Moutsopoulos, "Frangikes Ekklesies sten Hellada," no. 1, pp. 30–31, also mentions it as a Frankish addition.

94. Enlart, "Quelques monuments," p. 309, also compares the narthex to Pontigny, but he adds that its architecture is archaic and that it has the modesty of colonial buildings. He dates the addition of the portal to the beginning of the thirteenth century.

95. Enlart, "Manuel d'archéologie française," 2:538.

96. Stikas, "Stereosis," p. 24, says the portal was blocked up during the Turkish occupation.

97. Enlart, "Quelques monuments," p. 310, adds that one also finds this motif in Byzantine architecture.

98. Stikas, "Stereosis," p. 31.

99. Enlart, "Quelques monuments," p. 309, and Moutsopoulos, "Frangikes Ekklesies sten Hellada," p. 31.

100. As E. Lambert states in *L'art gothique en Espagne* (Paris, 1931), the Gothic style had been introduced in Spain by the Cistercians and the art of Burgundy and southern France developed in Spain in a new environment.

101. J. M. Canivez, "Daphni," in *Dictionnaire de l'histoire et de la géographie ecclesiastique*, 14:80.

102. Gregorovius, *Geschichte der Stadt Athen*, 2:65.

103. Ibid., p. 69.

104. Millet, *Daphni*, p. 40.

105. Stikas, "Stereosis," p. 33.

106. Millet, *Daphni*, pl. 5. 2.

107. Ibid., p. 38.

108. Ibid., also Stikas, "Stereosis," p. 30.

109. Buchon, *Grèce continentale*, pp. 131–33, found two sarcophagi.

110. Millet, *Daphni*, p. 40.

111. Brown, "Cistercians in the Latin Empire," p. 85.

112. "Petitio abbati sancti Thomas de Venetia qui petit quod possit mittere monachos suos in Cretam et ibidem secundum beati Benedicti regulam vivere valeant et secundum nostri ordinis disciplinam." Canivez, *Statuta*, 3, 122–23, no. 40.

Chapter Four

1. Janin, *Géographie écclésiastique,* p. 55. The minorites were established in Constantinople in 1220. About the establishment of the Dominicans the most ancient document dates from 1233. Ibid., p. 590. About the Franciscans, see also R. L. Wolff, "The Latin Empire of Constantinople and the Franciscans," *Traditio* 2(1944):221.

2. Dimier, *Moines bâtisseurs,* p. 148.

3. Meerseman, "Architecture dominicaine," 16(1946):139.

4. "Statuta generalia ordinis, edita in capitulis generalibus celebratis: Narbonnae, an. 1260, Assissii, an. 1279, atque Parisiis, an. 1292." *Archivo Franciscanum Historicum* 69:47, no. 19.

5. The biographers of Saint Dominic speak of no restrictions he imposed on the architecture of churches. It was the order that wanted to be content with low and small churches. Ibid., p. 147.

6. The Premonstratensians was a monastic order established by Saint Norbert in 1120 at Prémontré. It is related to the order of Saint Augustine.

7. Andravida (in Elis) existed even before the arrival of the Franks. It was also known by the names Antravita, Andravilla, and Andreville.

8. *Libro de los Fechos* (Geneva, 1895), p. 346.

9. Bon, *Morée Franque,* pp. 100, 319. Today this no longer exists.

10. G. Golubovitch, *Bibliotheca bio-bibliographica della Terra Santa e dell' oriente franciscano* (Florence, 196–13), 2:224, Wadding, *Annales minorum,* 2:206.

11. *Chronique grecque,* pp. 7417–20.

12. Traquair, "Frankish Architecture," p. 20, believes it dates from the end of the thirteenth century or the beginning of the fourteenth. Bon, *Morée Franque,* p. 547, places it a little before 1250.

13. Ibid.; Loenertz, "Documents," p. 73.

14. Rodd, Sir Rennell, *The Princes of Achaea and the Chronicle of Morea* (London, 1907), 2:174; Traquair, "Frankish Architecture," p. 17; Bon, *Morée Franque,* p. 548, n. 2, doubts that the columns of Lechaina came from Saint Sophia.

15. *Bulletin de Correspondance Héllenique* (1962), p. 749, reports on the reconstruction done at the time.

16. Traquair, "Frankish Architecture," p. 17.

17. Ibid.; Bon, *Morée Franque,* p. 548. Today this part of the wall is not visible. Saint Sophia suffered especially from the local people, who used the stones for their own buildings.

18. Ibid., p. 552.

19. Ibid., pl. 13*b, c.*

20. Ibid., pl. 11*a–b.*

21. Moutsopoulos, *Eglises franques,* p. 12, mistakes these capitals for brackets.

22. Aubert, *Architecture cistercienne,* p. 285.

23. Bon, *Morée Franque,* p. 551.

24. Meerseman, "Architecture dominicaine," p. 142.

25. Bon, *Morée Franque,* p. 553.

26. Ibid., pp. 551–52.

27. The church of Clarensia, not far from Andravida, was of the same plan. Bon studied it in 1925 and 1938. It was completely destroyed in 1941–44

during the occupation of the Germans, who razed the walls. Ibid., p. 559, fig. 7, p. 575.

28. Traquair, "Frankish architecture," p. 20.

29. Sotiriou, in Orlandos, *Mélanges Merlier*, 2:437; Bon, *Morée Franque*, pl. 21, *c–d*.

30. A. Orlandos, "Ai Vlachernai tes Eleias," *Archaiologike Efemeris* (1923), p. 34; Bon, *Morée Franque*, p. 561; *Chronique grecque*, p. 7518. The *Chronique* speaks of the "Moustier de St. François" where the court of the lords of Morea gathered. It is not quite clear if it refers to the church of Clarensia, which was of course larger, or to the monastery of Vlachernes.

31. A. Bon, "Art oriental et art occidental en Grèce au moyen âge," in *Mélanges offerts à K. Michalowski* (Warsaw, 1966), p. 299; also Bon, *Morée Franque*, p. 571.

32. These inscriptions are placed on the facade over the arches of the porch.

33. Ch. Bouras, "The Church of the Paleopanagia at Manolada," *Scientific Annual of the School of Technology of the Aristotle University of Thessaloniki* 4(1969):258; Orlandos, "Vyzantinoi Naoi tes Anatolikes Korinthias," *Archeion Vyzantinon Mnemeion tes Hellados* 1(1935):118; Bon, *Morée Franque*, pp. 584–85.

34. Bon, "Monuments d'art byzantin et d'art occidental dans le Peloponnèse au 18ᵉ siècle," *Mélanges Orlandos* 3:88, n. 5, mentions that this head reminds one of the cats' heads at Hagia Paraskevi at Geraki in Laconia.

35. Ibid.

36. Bon, *"Art oriental,"* p. 298; H. Megaw, "The Chronology of Some Middle-Byzantine Churches," *Annual of the British School at Athens* 32 (1931–32):90–130.

37. One could compare them with the capitals of the chapter house of Noirlac, which belong to the twelfth century.

38. Orlandos, "Vyzantinoi Naoi," pp. 53–90. Speaking of the Dormition of the Virgin in Corinth, he says that this type of vault exists in the twelfth century and is not Western. Bon, *Mélanges Merlier*, pp. 89–90, proposes that perhaps several churches of Corinth were built like the Palaiomonastiro of Phaneromeni at the beginning of the thirteenth century after the arrival of the Franks, when several Greek monks abandoned monasteries and found refuge far from the centers occupied by the Franks.

39. Traquair, "Frankish architecture," pp. 20 and 24. The principality was ruled by the Angevins 1278–1376.

40. Wadding, *Annales minorum*, p. 215, cites a document of 1246 for the dispatching of Franciscans to Syria, Cyprus, Armenia, and Crete. Wolff, "Latin Empire," p. 231, says the Franciscans established themselves in Corinth before 1261.

41. Traquair, "Frankish Architecture," p. 24. This relationship does not seem acceptable.

42. N. Tsirpanlis, "Nea Stoicheia Sketika me ten Ekklesiastiken Historian tes Venetokratoumenes Kretes (13os–17os aionas) apo Anekdota Venetika Engrafa," *Hellenika* 20(1967):42–106.

43. Fortunately, among the archives of Venice there still exists "l'archivio del Duca di Candia," a collection of Venetian documents covering the period between 1211 and 1669 in Crete. These official documents of the Venetian Cretan government were transported to Venice in 1669 by Fr. Moro-

sini and include 95 volumes. A small part of these have been published from time to time since the end of the nineteenth century. The published volumes do not include information on the construction of churches, which would be valuable for our study.

44. There are several isolated examples of sculptured portals or windows across Crete that Gerola had seen and that are typically Venetian of the fourteenth and fifteenth centuries. They must, however, be studied separately rather than included in this study, where the church plans are the major concern.

45. Jorga, "Documents concernant les Grecs et les affaires d'Orient tirés des régistres de notaires de Crète," *Revue Historique du Sud-Est Européen* 14(April–June 1937): 84–114. We have more information from the fifteenth century on: "1418—Frater Gaspar de Padua, prior monasterii et ecclesis fratrum predicatorum *Sancti Petri de Candia.* . . ."

46. Gerola, *Monumenti Veneti*, 2:126. In this monumental work Gerola presents the plans of 183 churches in Crete. Of these, 148 are small agrarian churches.

47. Restoration of Saint Peter was started in 1974 but is not yet completed.

48. E. Bertaux, *L'art de l'Italie méridionale* (Paris, 1904), p. 169. Stone pillars of this type that retain round arches were popular in southern Italy in the Romanesque period, especially in Benedictine churches.

49. Gerola, *Monumenti Veneti*, 2:126.

50. Gerola's plan shows this chapel as longer than it seems to be in reality.

51. Gerola, *Monumenti Veneti*, 2:127.

52. G. Hoffman, "La biblioteca scientifica del monastero di San Francesco di Candia nel medio-evo," *Orientalia Christiana Periodica* 8(1942):317–60. The library was one of the most famous and possessed important, often illuminated manuscripts. Three codices still exist in the archives of Venice.

53. Ibid., p. 111; Cornaro, *Creta Sacra*, 2:365.

54. Hoffman, "Biblioteca," 3:124, fig. 76.

55. The Crociferi were a monastic order related to the Augustinians. They wore wooden or metal or cloth crosses on their chests. The Crociferi of Italy were founded by Pope Alexander III in the twelfth century and were abolished by Pope Alexander VII in 1656.

56. Hoffman, "Biblioteca," 3:154.

57. Gerola, *Monumenti Veneti*, 2:128.

58. Papadakis, *He Ekklesia Kretes: Episkopai, Monai*, Greek and Latin churches at Candia during this period. Cornaro, *Creta Sacra*, 1:229–31; in his list of churches at Candia in 1658, Cornaro enumerates eleven small Latin churches and ten monasteries.

59. Thiriet, *Romanie vénitienne*, p. 286.

60. Gerola, *Monumenti Veneti*, 3:148. Marco Boschini, *Il regno tutto de Candia* (Venice, 1651), indicates these churches in his drawings, done just before the Turkish occupation.

61. Gerola, *Monumenti Veneti*, 2:134–35.

62. The plan of Gerola, (vol. 2, fig. 85) is not correct.

63. Ibid., 2:134.

64. *Bulletin de Correspondance Héllenique* (1962), p. 749.

65. Gerola, *Monumenti Veneti*, 3:149.

66. Onario Belli writes a letter in 1596 in which he talks of the restorations

made at this period, especially of the bell tower, which was taller before. *Bibl. Ambrosiana di Milano*, R. 122 (See Gerola, *Monumenti Veneti*, 2:132, n. 1).

67. The Service of Greek Restorations opened a door and a window in this eastern side. They reinforced the walls and the vaults, which were dangerously unstable in Gerola's time. Also, a marble floor was added. *Bulletin de Correspondance Héllenique* (1962), p. 749.

68. Boschini, *Regno Tutto di Candia*.

69. R. Branner, *St. Louis and the Court Style in Gothic Architecture* (London, 1965).

70. Enlart, *Art gothique en Chypre*, 1:202.

71. Francis, *Churches of Cyprus*, p. 48.

72. Traquair, "Frankish Architecture," p. 10. There is, however, no proof that these bases came from there.

73. C. Enlart, *L'architecture gothique en Italie* (Paris, 1893), p. 280.

74. Ibid., p. 215.

75. Francis, *Church of Cyprus*, p. 51.

76. Aubert, *Architecture cistercienne*, p. 264, gives as an example Beaulieu (Tarn and Garonne).

77. Enlart, *Architecture gothique en Italie*, p. 231.

78. Ibid., fig. 129.

79. Enlart, Art gothique en Chypre, 1:235.

80. Branner, *St. Louis*, p. 86.

81. L. K. Little, "St. Louis Involvement with the Friars," *Church History*, vol. 33 (1964).

82. Francis, *Churches of Cyprus*, p. 53.

83. Enlart, *Art gothique en Chypre*, 1:332.

84. "Statuta generalia ordinis, edita in capitulis generalibus celebratis, Narbonnae, an. 1260, Assissii, an. 1279, atque Parisiis, an. 1292," *Archivio Franciscanum Historicum* 34:47, no. 17.

85. Mas Latrie, M. L. de, *Histoire de l'Ile de Chypre sous le règne des princes de Lusignan*, (Paris, 1841), 2:187.

86. Francis, *Churches of Cyprus*, p. 40.

87. Enlart, *Art gothique en Chypre*, 1:335.

Chapter Five

1. Durliat, *Royaume de Majorque*, p. 116.

2. N. Giannopoulos, "Christianika kai Vyzantina Glypta Chalkidos," *Deltion Christianikes Archaiologikes Hetaireias* 1(1924):116–17. .

3. N. Kalogeropoulos, "Palaiochristianika kai Vyzantina Mnemeia kai Techne en Euvoia," extract from *Nea Hestia* (Athens, 1936), p. 12; Longnon, "*Henri de Valenciennes*" extract from *Journal des Savants*, 1945, pp. 134–50; Gregorovius, *Geschichte der Stadt Athen*, 2:22.

4. M. Coronelli, *Historia del regno di Negreponte et sue isole adjacenti* (Venice, 1695), map after p. 208.

5. J. Koder, *Negreponte: Untersuchungen und Siedlungsgeschichte der Insel Euboia während der Zeit der Venezianerherrschaft* (Vienna, 1973), p. 92. J. Strygowski, "Palaia Vyzantine Vasilike en Chalkidi," *Deltion tes Historikes kai Ethnologikes Hetaireias tes Hellados* 2(1885):711–28. Considers Saint

Paraskevi the most important church of Chalkis in the Venetian period. Moutsopoulos, "Frangikes Ekklesies sten Hellada," p. 20, mentions Spon and Wheeler, who had read an inscription in the court of the old palace of the Venetian bailie that spoke of the construction of the church of Saint Mark by the bailie.

6. Koder, *Negreponte*, p. 91.

7. Ibid., p. 143.

8. Letters of Pope Innocent III, ep. XI, 250 (pl. 215, 1555).

9. Soteriou, *Christianike kai Vyzantine Archaiologia* (Athens, 1942), 1:296. Strygowski, "Vasilike en Chalkidi," dates these columns a little later, in Justinian's period.

10. A. Xyngopoulos, "To Templon tes Hagias Paraskeves en Chalkidi," *Deltion tes Christianikes Archaiologikes Hetaireias* 4(1927):73. See also Giannopoulos, "Glypta Chalkidos," p. 116–17.

11. Soteriou, *Archeologia*, p. 296.

12. Traquair, "Frankish architecture," p. 11.

13. A. Didron, "Voyage archéologique dans la Grèce chrétienne," *Annales Archéologiques* 1(1844):52, says that Saint Paraskevi was completely vaulted. This does not seem possible, and Lambakis, in *Hebdomas*, 1:267, insists that the sloping wooden roof dates from the Frankish period. Didron, who visited the church before the last reconstruction of the western side, mentions that he saw seven bays. He must have counted in the choir.

14. Traquair, "Frankish architecture," p. 14.

15. Enlart, "Quelques monuments," p. 311.

16. Xyngopoulos, "Templon," pp. 67–74.

17. Saint Mark appears on several seventeenth-century maps; see Marco Boschini, Giorgio Cornaro (Corner), Buondelmonte, Giorgio Clonza. Their drawings are naturally too schematic to let us recognize the plan of Saint Mark and the details of its bell tower with the crenellations, on which always fluttered the flag of Saint Mark the Evangelist.

18. G. Gerola, "Una descrizione di Candia del principio del seicento" *Atti dell J. R. Accademia di Scienza, Letteri et Arti degli Agiati, Roverto* 14, 3 and 4 (1908).

19. Gerola, *Monumenti Veneti*, 2:17.

20. St. Alexiou and C. Lassithiotakis, *He Apokatastasis tou Naou tou Hagiou Markou tou Handakos* (Herakleion, Crete, 1958), p. 12.

21. Ibid. These paintings were Byzantine, as were those that covered the walls of the churches of the monasteries of Saint Francis of Candia, Saint Peter Martyr, and Saint Mary of the Crusaders.

22. Gerola, *Monumenti Veneti*, 2:19, note 4.

23. Alexiou, *Hagios Markos*, p. 13.

24. The appearance of the church is known from the drawing of Cornaro in 1625.

25. Alexiou, *Hagios Markos*, p. 13.

26. Enlart, *Architecture gothique en Italie*, p. 321.

27. Francis, *Churches of Cyprus*, p. 39.

28. Enlart, *Architecture gothique en Italie*, pp. 321, 325.

29. Ibid., p. 327.

30. Its history is little known. It has served as a monastic and parochial church.

Conclusion

1. Ch. Bouras, *Vyzantina Stavrotholia me Nevroseis* (Athens, 1965), p. 68.

2. Bon, "Art Oriental et Art Occidental," p. 298.

3. Ch. Bouras, "Dyo Mikroi Naoi Oktagonikou typou, Anekdotoi," *Deltion Christianikes Archaiologikes Hetaireias*, ser. D, 3(1962):140.

4. Megaw, "Chronology of Some Middle-Byzantine Churches," 32:114, 129.

5. Orlandos, *He Omorfe Ekklesia* (Athens, 1921), p. 17, had dated it to the thirteenth century, but according to Bouras and Megaw this chapel is from the end of the twelfth century.

6. A. Couchaud, *Choix d'églises byzantines* (Paris, 1842), fig. 6.

7. Bon, *Morée Franque*, pp. 578–80.

8. Ibid., pp. 581–82, fig. 9. Traquair, "Frankish architecture," pp. 26–27, fig. 31.

9. Bon, *Morée Franque*, p. 584.

10. A. J. B. Wace, "Frankish Sculpture at Parori, Geraki," *Annual of the British School of Archaeology* 11:140–45.

11. Traquair, "Medieval Fortresses of Northwestern Peloponnesus, *Annual of the British School of Archaeology* 13(1906–7):268–81.

12. Bon, *Morée Franque*, pp. 592–98.

13. Orlandos, "Ta Palatia kai ta Spitia tou Mystra," *Archeion ton Vyzantinon Mnemeion tes Hellados* (1937), 3:32.

14. Enlart "Quelques monuments," p. 311.

15. Gerola, *Monumenti Veneti*, 2:263.

16. A. Orlandos, "Mesaionika Mnemeia Oropou kai Sykaminou," *Deltion Christianikes Archaiologikes Hetaireias*, ser. B, issue 4(1927):25–45.

17. A. Orlandos, *He Paregoritissa tes Artes* (Athens, 1963), pp. 66–71.

Glossary

Abacus. A slab between the capital of a column and an arch or lintel.

Aisles. The sides of a church nave separated by piers from the nave proper.

Apse. The east or altar end of a church or chapel and the termination of the choir; usually semicircular or polygonal.

Arcade. A series of arches supported on piers or columns. A blind arcade is placed against a wall as a decorative feature.

Arch. A typically curved structural member spanning an opening and serving as a support for the wall or other weight above it.

BLIND ARCH. An arch with no opening, or a relieving arch concealed behind a wall facing.

OGEE OR OGIVAL ARCH. A pointed arch, usually with four arcs, the center two inside the arch and the other two outside. This results in a curve of two parts, one convex and the other concave.

POINTED ARCH. An arch produced by two curves, each with a radius equal to the span of the arch, meeting in a point at the top.

RELIEVING ARCH. An arch constructed within the masonry to help carry the weight of its superstructure by channeling the weight to fixed points at the extremities of the arch.

ROUND ARCH. Wedge-shaped blocks of masonry arranged in a semicircle.

TRANSVERVE ARCH. An arch spanning a barrel vault.

Archivolt. The undersurface of an arch; sometimes used as a synonym for voussoirs. Also, an ornamental molding around the outer surface of an arch.

Ashlar. A thin squared and dressed stone used for facing a wall of rubble or brick.

Assomoir. A deadfall trap.

Attic base. A molded base consisting of an upper and lower torus separated by a scotia and two narrow fillets.

Basilica. A Latin-cross church whose nave is higher than the aisles.

Bastion. A bulwark projecting from a fortified building.

Bay. A division of the layout of a building marked not by walls but by pilasters, arcading, and very often vaulting over each bay.

Beaded molding. A small salient molding of rounded surface, continuous or broken.

Boss. A projecting keystone placed at the intersection of ribs in a vault, usually with a sculptured decoration.

Buttress. A projecting mass of masonry used to strengthen a wall; usually placed at right angles to the building, but occasionally placed diagonally.

Cavetto. A concave molding having a curve that roughly approximates a quarter-circle.

Chamfer molding. A grooved molding.

Chevron. A zigzag ornament made of short lines intersecting at an angle; usually seen in Anglo-Norman architecture.

Chapel. A room or recess in a church for meditation and prayer or small religious services.

Chancel. The part of a church containing the altar and seats for the clergy and choir.

Choir. The east end of a church interior used for seating trained singers or for the chanting of the services; almost synonymous with chancel.

Clerestory. The windows in the upper walls of the nave, projecting above the aisles.

Cloister. A vaulted, paved walk, open on one side, around a square adjoining an abbey or cathedral church.

Colonnade. A range of columns.

Colonnette. A small column of secondary use.

Console. A classical form of corbel with scrolls and volutes.

Corbel. A projecting bracket on a wall to carry weight.

Cornice. A projecting decorative molding along the top of a wall or arch.

Coupled columns. Double shafts used in place of a single column.

Crenellations. Repeated indentations like those in a battlement.

Crockets. Sculptured flowers or buds arranged at regular intervals.

Crossing. The intersection of nave, transept, and choir.

Cupola. A semicircular or polygonal domed vault.

Cusp. An ornamental pointed projection (as from the intrados of a Gothic arch) formed by the intersection of two arcs or foils.

Dormitory. A sleeping room in a monastery, containing many beds.

Dripstone. A part of a horizontal architectural member that projects beyond the rest so as to throw off rainwater.

Elevation. A geometrical projection of a building on a vertical plane.

Enceinte. A line of fortification enclosing a castle or town.

Engaged column. A quarter, half, or three-quarter column attached to a pier or wall to support the ribs or transverse arches of a vaulting system. Several engaged columns grouped around a pier, disguising the core, constitute a cluster pier.

Extrados. The outer or upper curve of an arch.

Facade. The front of a building.

Fillet. A flat molding separating other moldings.

Finial. A usually foliated ornament crowning an upper extremity such as the peak of a gable.

Fluting. Decorative parallel grooves.

Foil. One of several small curved indentations that meet and form points; an indentation between cusps in Gothic tracery.

Formeret. *See* Ribs.

Fret. A geometrical ornament of horizontal and vertical straight lines repeated to form a band.

Groin. The line of intersection of two vaulted surfaces.

Iconostasis. A screen in a Byzantine church placed between the sanctuary and the nave.

Impost. The molding on which an arch rests.

Interlace. A geometric crisscross pattern.

Intrados. The interior or lower curve of an arch.

Jamb. The sides of a window or door cut diagonally into the wall.

Keystone. The central wedge-shaped stone at the top of an arch or vault that locks the others in place.

Lancet. A slender window ending in an acutely pointed arch.

Light. An opening between the mullions of a window.

Lintel. A horizontal block of stone or beam placed over the opening of a doorway or window, supporting the wall above.

Loggia. A roofed open gallery, especially at an upper story overlooking an open court.

Nihrab. A niche or chamber in a mosque indicating the direction of Mecca and usually containing a copy of the Koran; sometimes only a slab used to indicate the direction.

Minaret. A slender tower on a mosque from which the faithful are called to prayer.

Molding. A decorative plane or curved strip used for ornamentation or finishing.

Mullion. An upright shaft dividing a window into lights.

Naos. In Byzantine architecture, the sanctuary of a centrally planned church.

Narthex. A large enclosed porch or vestibule at the west entrance of a church.

Nave. The long, narrow central hall in a cruciform church, flanked by the aisles.

Nave arcade. The arcade dividing the nave from the aisles.

Nymphaeum. A room or niche built in antiquity as a sanctuary for nymphs, usually containing water, flowers, and sculpture.

Oculus. A round opening or window without stone tracery.

Palmette. An ornamental motif in the shape of a palm leaf.

Pediment. A triangular space forming the gable of a two-pitched roof, or a similar form used as a decoration.

Pier. An upright support of solid masonry, usually square but sometimes circular to look like a column.

Pilaster. A decorative vertical strip attached to the wall surface to look like a thin pillar; a shallow engaged column.

Piscina. A basin with a drain near the altar of a church for disposing of water from liturgical ablutions.

Plinth. The projecting base block of a wall or column.

Podium. A pedestal or base of masonry on which a building rests.

Portal. A principal doorway or entrance.

Portico. A colonnaded entrance porch.

Proskynitari. *See* Iconostasis.

Quatrefoil. A geometric pattern with four lobes like a four-leaf clover.

Rayonnant. The style of French Gothic between 1250 and 1350, characterized by large windows with radiating linear tracery.

Refectory. The dining room of a monastery.

Ribs. The supporting or articulating frame of a groined vault.

TRANSVERSE RIB. A rib crossing the space to be vaulted at a right angle to the axis.

FORMERET OR WALL RIB. A rib at the intersection of vault and wall, next to the wall and shorter than the other ribs.

Roof, lean to. A roof with one inclined surface.

Rosette. A round floral boss with radiating petals.

Sacristy. A room in a church where sacred vestments and other valuable objects are kept and where the clergy enrobe.

Salient. Projecting outward or upward from the background.

Sanctuary. The most sacred part of a church, where the altar is placed.

Scotia. A concave molding used in the bases of columns.

Spandrel. A triangular space between the curves of two adjacent arches.

Stringcourse. A horizontal molding band dividing one register from another.

Tas-de-charge. The portion of a group of vault ribs that occurs just above the spring where the ribs are still joined together.

Torus. A large molding of convex semicircular profile, usually found just above the plinth of a column base.

Tracery. Ornamental ribwork of stone used as a frame for glass in a window or as a decorative pattern on an open space of wall.

Trefoil. A three-lobed geometric figure like a stylized trifoliate leaf.

Triforium. An arcaded wall passage opening on the nave and placed between the nave arches and clerestory.

Tufa. Rough porous stone formed as a deposit from springs or streams.

Tympanum. The space within an arch and above a lintel or a subordinate arch.

Undercroft. A vaulted chamber under a church.

Vault. An arched masonry ceiling.

BARREL VAULT. A continuous half-cylinder vault unbroken by ribs or groins.

HALF BARREL VAULT. An asymmetrical vault whose section is a quadrant.

GROIN VAULT. Two barrel vaults intersecting at right angles.

RAMPANT VAULT. A vault having one impost or abutment higher than the other.

RIBBED VAULT. A vault in which a framework of solid ribs supports the vaulted surface.

Volute. A spiral, scroll-shaped ornament on a capital.

Voussoirs. The wedge-shaped stones composing an arch.

Window embrasure. The chamfered edge of a window opening.

Bibliography

Adamantiou, A. "Ta Chronika tou Moreos" [The chronicles of Morea]. *Deltion tes Historikes kai Ethnologikes Hetaireias tes Hellados* 6 (1901–6): 453–670.

Alexiou, St., and Lassithiotakis, C. *He Apokatastasis tou Naou tou Hagiou Markou tou Handakos* [The restoration of the church of Saint Mark of Handax]. Herakleion, Crete, 1958.

Altaner, Berthold. *Die Dominikanermissionen des 13 Jahrhunderts.* Habelschwardt Schlesien, 1924.

Archivo Franciscanum Historicum (Collegium S. Bonaventura Quaracci, Italy, 1908).

Argenti, Philip. *The Occupation of Chios by the Genoese and Their Administration of the Island: 1346–1566.* 3 vols. Cambridge, 1953.

Aubert, M. *Architecture cistercienne en France.* 2 vols. Paris, 1943.

———. "Existe-t-il une architecture cistercienne?" *Cahiers de Civilisation Mediévale* 1 (1958):153–58 (Poitiers, France).

Auvray, L. *Les registres de Gregoire IX.* 2 vols. Paris, 1907. Bacchion, Eugenio. *Il dominio Veneto su Corfu: 1386–1797.* Venice, 1956.

Beer, J. M. A. *Villehardouin: Epic Historian.* Etudes de Philologie et d'Histoire. Geneva, 1968.

Bennett, R. F. *The Early Dominicans: Studies in Thirteenth Century Dominican History.* Cambridge, 1937.

Bertaux, E. *L'art de l'Italie méridionale.* Paris, 1904.

Bilson, J. "The Architecture of the Cistercians." *Archaeological Journal* (London, 1909).

Bistori, Giulio. *La Repubblica di Venezia della transmigrationi nelle laguna fino alle caduta di Constantinopoli 1453.* Venice, 1916.

Blouet, A. *Architecture, sculpture, inscriptions et vues du Peloponnèse, des Cyclades et de l'Attique.* Publication Expedition Scientifique de Morée. 3 vols. Paris: Firmin Didot Frères, 1831–38.

Boase, T. S. R. *Castles and Churches of the Crusading Kingdom.* London, 1967.

Boetticher, A. "Die frankischen Bauten in Morea." *Beilage zur Allgemeine Zeitung.* Munich, 1885.

Bolton, Brenda M. "A Mission to the Orthodox? The Cistercians in Romania." In *The Orthodox Churches and the West: Studies in Church History,* edited by D. Baker, 13 (1976):169–81.

Bon, A. "Art oriental et art occidental en Grèce au moyen âge." *Mélanges offerts à K. Michalowski.* Warsaw, 1966.

————. "Monuments d'art byzantin et d'art occidental dans le Peloponnèse, au 13e siècle." *Mélanges offerts à Orlandos,* "Haristerion eis A. K. Orlandon" [Studies offered to A. K. Orlandos]. *Library of the Archeological Society of Athens,* no. 54, 3 (1965–66):86–93.

————. "Monuments vénitiens en Grèce centrale et dans le Peloponnèse jusqu'au 15e siècle." In *Venezia e il Levante fino al secolo 15,* ed. A. Pertusi, vol. 2. Florence, 1974.

————. *La Morée Franque: Recherches historiques, topographiques et archéologiques sur la principauté d'Achaie (1205–1430).* Paris, 1969.

————. *Le Peloponnèse byzantin jusqu'en 1204.* Paris, 1951.

Boschini, Marco. *Il regno tutto di Candia.* Venice, 1651.

Bouras, Ch. "The Church of Paleopanagia at Manolada." *Scientific Annual of the School of Technology of the Aristotle University of Thessaloniki* 4 (1969):258.

————. "Dyo Mikroi Naoi Oktagonikou Typou: Anekdotoi" [Two small churches of the octagonal type: Unpublished]. *Deltion Christianikes Archaelogikes Hetaireias,* ser. D, 3 (1962):140.

————. *Vyzantina Stavrotholia me Nevroseis* [Byzantine ribbed vaults]. Athens, 1965.

Brand, C. M. *Byzantium Confronts the West: 1180–1204.* Cambridge, Mass., 1968.

Branner, R. *Burgundian Gothic Architecture.* London, 1960.

————. "Paris and the Origins of Rayonnant Gothic Architecture down to 1240." *Art Bulletin* 48 (March 1962):39.

————. *St. Louis and the Court Style in Gothic Architecture.* London, 1965.

Braunfels, Wolfgang. *Monasteries of Western Europe.* Princeton: Princeton University Press, 1972.

Brown, Elizabeth A. R. "The Cistercians in the Latin Empire of Constantinople and Greece." *Traditio* 14 (1958):63–120 (New York: Fordham University Press).

Bucher, F. *Zisterzienserabtei: Notre Dame de Bonmont.* Bern, 1957.

Buchon, J. A. C. *Atlas des nouvelles recherches historiques sur la principauté française de Morée.* Paris, 1845.

————. *Chroniques étrangères relatives aux expéditions françaises pendant le 18e siècle.* 2 vols. Paris, 1840.

————. *La Grèce continentale et la Morée: Voyages, séjour et études historiques en 1840, 1841, 1843.* Paris, 1843.

————. *Recherches et matériaux pour servir à l'histoire de la domination française aux 13e, 14e et 15e siècles dans les provinces demembrées de l'empire grec à la suite de la 4eme croisade.* 2 vols. Paris, 1840.

————. *Recherches historiques sur la principauté française de Morée et ses hautes baronies.* 2 vols. Paris, 1845.

Burnouf, E. *La ville de l'acropole d'Athènes au diverses époques.* Paris, 1877.

Bury, J. B. "The Lombards and Venetians in Euboea." *Journal of Hellenic Studies* 7 (1886):326–28.

Bustron, Florio. "Chronique de l'Ile de Chypre." In *Melanges historiques: Choix de documents,* vol. 5. Paris: Mashatril, 1869.

Canivez, J. M. "Daphni." *Dictionnaire de l'histoire et de la géographie ecclesiastique* 14:80 (Paris).

————. *Les statua selecta capitulorum generalium ordinis Cisterciensis, ab anno 1116 ad annum 1786.* Louvain, 1933–41.

Clair, R. "Les filles de Hautecombe dans l'empire latin de Constantinople." *Analecta Sacri Ordinis Cisterciensis* 17 (1961):262–68.

Clara Rhodos. *Studi e materiali publicati a cura dell Istituto Storico-Archeologicco di Rodi.* Vol. 8. Rhodes, 1928–41.

Cessi, Roberto. *Storia della Repubblica di Venezia.* Milan, 1944.

Chambers, D. S. *The Imperial Age of Venice: 1380–1580.* London, 1970.

Chronicle of Morea: different versions—Aragonese, French, Greek, and Italian:

    Hopf, C., ed. *Cronaca di Morea.* Berlin, 1873.

    Longnon, J., ed. *Livre de la conquête de la princée de l'Amorée.* Paris, 1911.

    Morel-Fatio, A., ed. *Libro de los Fechos.* Geneva, 1895.

    Schmitt, J., ed. *The Chronicle of Morea: A History in Political Verse, Relating the Establishment of Feudalism in Greece by the Franks in the Twelfth Century.* London, 1904. Reproduced by M. Kolonaros, ed., *Ta chronika tou Moreos.* Athens, 1940.

Clari, Robert de. *La conquête de Constantinople.* In *Les classiques français du moyen âge,* ed. Ph. Lauer, vol. 40. Paris, 1924.

Cornaro, Flaminio [also Cornelius, Corner]. *Crete Sacra.* 2 vols. Venice, 1755.

————. *Ecclesiae Torcellanae antiquis monumentis illustratae.* Vol. 1. Venice, 1749.

Coronelli, M. *Historia del regno di Negreponte e sue isole adjacenti.* Venice, 1695.

————. *Memorie istoriografiche delli regni della Morea: Negreponte e luoghi adjacenti.* Venice, 1685.

Couchaud, A. *Choix d'églises byzantines.* Paris, 1842.

Dalieggio, d'Alesio. *Erevnai peri ton Latinikon Ekklesion kai Monon ton Athenon epi Tourkokratias* [Researches on the Latin churches and monasteries of Athens during the Turkish occupation]. Athens, 1964.

Dapper, O. *Description exacte des îles de l'Archipel.* Amsterdam, 1703.

Dawkins, Richard McG., and Wace, Alan J. B. "Notes from the Sporades." *Annual of the British School of Athens* 12 (1905–6):152.

De Dion, A. "Notes sur l'architecture de l'ordre de Grandmont." *Bulletin Monumental.* Paris: Société Française d'Archéologie, 1874.

Dellaville le Roux, J. *Les Hospitaliers à Rhodes jusqu'a la mort de Philibert de Naillac (1310–1421).* Paris, 1913.

Didron, Aine. "Voyage archéologique dans la Grèce chrétienne." *Annales Archéologiques,* vol. 1 (Paris, 1844).

Diehl, Charles. *La république de Venise.* Paris, 1967.

Dimier, A. *Les moines bâtisseurs.* Paris, 1964.

————. *Recueil de plans d'églises cisterciennes.* Paris, 1949.

Dodwell, E. *A Classical and Topographical Tour through Greece during the Years 1801, 1805, and 1806.* 2 vols. London, 1819.

Dragoumes, St. *Chronikon tou Moreos: Toponymika, Topographika, Historika.* Athens, 1921.

Du Cange, Charles du Fresne. *Histoire de l'empire de Constantinople sous les empereurs français*, ed. J. A. C. Buchon. In *Collections de chroniques nationales écrites en langue vulgaire du 13ᵉ et 14ᵉ siècle*. Vols. 1 and 2. Paris, 1826.

Duhn, F. von. "Eine Ansicht der Acropolis aus dem Jahre 1670." In *Mitteilungen des Deutschen Archaeologischen Institutes in Athen*, pp. 38–47. Athens, 1877.

Durand, U., and Martène, E. *Thesaurus nuovum anecdotorum*. Vol. 4, Paris, 1717.

Durliat, M. *L'art dans le royaume de Majorque*. Paris, 1962.

Enlart, C. "L'architecture gothique en Italie." Paris, 1893 (reprinted from Revue Archéologique).

———. *L'art gothique et la Renaissance en Chypre*. Paris, 1899.

———. "Manuel d'archéologie française." In *Architecture religieuse*, vol. 1. Paris, 1919.

———. *Origines françaises de l'architecture gothique en Italie*. Paris, 1894.

———. "Quelques monuments d'architecture gothique en Grèce." *Revue de l'Art Chrétien*, 4th ser., 8 (1897):309–14. Lille, France.

Eydoux, A. P. *Eglises cisterciennes d'Allemagne*. Paris, 1952.

Fedalto, G. *La chiesa latina in Oriente*. Studi religiosi, vol. 1. Verona, 1973.

Focillon, H. *The Art of the West*. 2 vols. London, 1963.

Francis, R. B. *The Medieval Churches of Cyprus*. London, 1949.

Gabriel, A. *La cité de Rhodes: Architecture et topographie militaire, architecture civile et religieuse*. Paris, 1921.

Gautier, J. *Les inscriptions des abbayes cisterciennes du diocèse de Besançon*. Besançon, 1882.

———. *Othon de la Roche conquérant d'Athènes et sa famille. Matériaux archéologiques inédits*. Besançon: Academie des Sciences, Belles-Lettres et Arts de Besançon, 1880.

Geanakoplos, D. J. "Bonaventura: The Two Mendicant Orders and the Greeks at the Council of Lyon (1274)." In *One yet Two*, ed. D. Geanakoplos, pp. 183–211. Kalamazoo, Mich.: Cistercian Publications, 1976.

———. *Emperor Michael Paleologus and the West, 1258–1282: A Study of Byzantine-Latin Relations*. Cambridge, Mass., 1959.

Gerland, E. *Erzbistums von Patras, Neue Quellen zur Geschichte des Lateinischen Erzbistums von Patras*. Leipzig, 1903.

Gerola, G. "Una descrizione di Candia del principio del seicento." *Atti dell I. R. Accademia di Scienza, Letteri et Arti degli Agiati, Rovereto*, ser. 3, vol. 14 (1908), fascs. 3 and 4.

———. *I monumenti Veneti nell' Isola di Creta*. Venice, 1908–38.

Giannopoulos, N. I. "Christian Antiquities of Chalkis." In *Deltion Historikes kai Ethnologikes Hetaireias Hellados*, vol. 9. Athens, 1926.

———. "Christianika kai Vyzantina Glypta Chalkidos" [Christian and Byzantine sculptures of Chalkis]. In *Deltion Christianikes Archaiologikes Hetaireias*, 1:116–17. Athens, 1924.

Golubovitch, G. *Bibliotheca bio-bibliographica della Terra Sante e dell' oriente franciscano*. 3 vols. Florence, 1906–19.

Gratien, P. *La fondation et l'évolution de l'ordre des Frères Mineurs au 13ᵉ siècle*. Paris, 1928.

Gregorovius, F. *Geschichte der Stadt Athen im Mittelalter*. Vols. 1 and 2. Stuttgart, 1889.

Gross, W. *Die abendländische Architektur um 1300*. Stuttgart, 1948.

Hadjidakis, M. *Mystras*. Athens, 1948.

Hadjipanou, P. V. "He Euboia kata ten Frangokratian" [Euboia during the Frankish occupation]. *Archeion Euboikon Meleton* 1 (1935):24.

Hamilton, Bernard. "The Cistercians in the Crusade States." In *One yet Two*, ed. D. Geanakoplos, pp. 405–22. Kalamazoo, Mich.: Cistercian Publications, 1976.

Hasluck, F. W. "Chios." *Burlington Magazine* 18 (1910–11): 329 (London).

———. "The Latin Monuments of Chios." *Annual of the British School at Athens* 16 (1909–10):157.

Helyot, P. "Dictionnaire des ordres religieux." Edited by M. L. Badiche. In *Encyclopédie theologique*, ed. J. P. Migne, vols. 20–23. Paris, 1847–59.

Hill, Sir George. *History of Cyprus*. 3 vols. Cambridge, 1948.

Hoffman, G. "La biblioteca scientifica del monastero di San Francesco di Candia nel medio-evo." *Orientalia Christiana Periodica* 8 (1942):317–60 (Rome: Pontificio Istituto Orientale).

Hopf, Charles. "Frankische Zeit von der Eroberung Konstantinoples durch die Kreuzfahrer bis zur Vernichtung der occidentalischen Feudalstaaten durch die Turken." Part of "Geschichte Griechenlands vom Begin des Mittlalters bis auf unsere Zeit." In *Allgemeine Encyclopedie der Wissenschaften und Künste*, ed. Ersch and Gruber. Leipzig, 1867–68.

Innocent III. *Epistolae 13*. In *Patrologie latine de Migne*, vol. 216. Paris, 1855.

Janauschek, L. *Originum Cisterciensium*. Vols. 1 and 2. Venice, 1877.

Janin, R. *La géographie écclésiastique de l'empire byzantin: Le siège de Constantinople et le patriarcat oecumenique: Les églises, les monastères*. Part 1, vol. 3. Paris, 1953.

Jeffreys, M. "Formulas in the Chronicle of the Morea." *Dumbarton Oaks Papers*, no. 227 (1973), pp. 163–95.

Jorga, N. "Documents concernant les Grecs et les affaires d'Orient tirés des régistres de notaires de Crète." *Revue Historique du Sud-Est Européen* 14 (April–June 1937):84–114 (Bucharest).

Judeich, W., ed. "Athen im Jahre 1395 nach der Beschreibung des Niccolo da Martoni." *Mitteilugen des Deutschen Archaeologischen Institutes in Athen* (1897), pp. 425–38.

Julleville, Petit de. "Recherches sur l'emplacement et le vocable des églises chrétiennes en Grèce." *Archives des Missions* 13 (1868):492.

Kalogeropoulos, N. D. "Palaiochristianika kai Vyzantina Mnemeia kai Techne en Euboia" [Early Christian and Byzantine monuments and art in Euboia]. In *Nea Hestia*. Athens, 1936.

Kambouroglou, D. *Old Athens*. Athens, 1922.

Koder, Johannes. *Negreponte: Untersuchungen und Siedlungsgeschichte der Insel Euboia während der Zeit der Venezianerherrschaft*. Vienna, 1973.

Krautcheimer, R. *Die Kierchen der Bettleorden in Deutschland*. Cologne, 1925.

Kretschmayer, Heinrich. *Geschichte von Venedig*. 3 vols. Gotha, 1905–20.

Lambakis, G. "He en Chalkidi Vasilike tes Hagias Paraskeves" [The basilica of Hagia Paraskeve in Chalkis]. *Hebdomas*, nos. 4–10, 34 (1884):267–68.

———. "Palaia Panagia sten Manolada" [Palaia Panagia in Manolada]. In *Deltion Christinikes Archaiologikes Hetaireias* (1894), pp. 14 and 15; (1900), p. 89.

Lambert, E. *l'art gothique en Espagne*. Paris, 1931.

Lane, Frederic C. *Venice: A Maritime Republic*. Baltimore, 1973.

Lavedan, P. *L'architecture gothique religieuse en Catalogne, Valence et Baleares*. Paris, 1935.

Leake, W. M. *Peloponnesiaca*. London, 1846.

———. *Travels in the Morea*. 3 vols. London, 1830.

Lenoir, A. *Architecture monastique: Documents inédits*. Paris, 1856.

Lenormant, Fr. "Le monastère de Daphni près d'Athènes sous la domination des princes croisés." *Revue Archéologique* (Paris, 1872).

Leonard, E. G. *Les Angevins de Naples*. Paris, 1954.

Little, Lester K. "St. Louis Involvement with Friars." *Church History*, vol. 33 (1964) (Wallingford, Pa.: American Society of Church History).

Loenertz, R. "Documents pour servir à l'histoire de la province dominicaine de Grèce, 1474–1669." *Archivum Fratrum Praedicatorum* 14 (1944): 74 (Rome: Istituto Storico Domenicano).

———. "Les établissements dominicains de Pera-Constantinople." *Echos d'Orient*, vol. 34 (1933). (Paris, 1897–1943).

———. "Marino Dandolo et son conflit avec l'évêque Jean." *Orientalia Christiana Periodica* 25 (1959):169 (Rome: Pontificio Istituto Orientale).

———. "Les seigneurs tierciers de Négrepont de 1205–80." *Byzantion* 35 (1965):235 (Brussels).

Longnon, Jean. "Le chroniqueur Henri de Valenciennes." *Journal des Savants* (1945), pp. 134–50 (Paris).

———. *Documents relatifs à l'histoire des Croisades*. Paris, 1948.

———. *L'empire latin de Constantinople et la principauté de Morée*. Paris, 1949.

———. *Les Français d'outre-mer au moyen âge: Essai sur l'expansion française dans le bassin de la Mediterranée*. Paris, 1929.

———. "Problèmes de l'histoire de la principauté de Morée." *Journal des Savants* (1946), pp. 178–85 (Paris).

———. *Recherches sur la vie de Geoffrey de Villehardouin suivies du catalogue des actes de Villehardouin*. Paris, 1939.

Luchaire, M. *Innocent III et la question de l'Orient*. Paris, 1907.

McNeil, William. *Venice: The Hinge of Europe, 1081–1797*. Chicago, 1974.

Magliano, Panfilo da. *Storia universale della missioni Franciscani*. Vols. 3 and 4.

Manrique, Angel. *Cistercienses sue verius ecclesiastici annales a condito Cistercio*. 4 vols. Lyons, 1642–59.

Mas Latrie, M. L. de. *Histoire de l'Ile de Chypre sous le règne des princes de Lusignan*. Vol. 2. Paris, 1841.

Meer, F. van der. *Atlas de l'ordre cistercien*. Haarlem, 1965.

Meerseman, R. P. "L'architecture dominicaine du 13ᵉ siècle: Legislation et pratique." *Archivum Fratrum Praedicatorum* 16 (1946):136–90 (Rome: Istituto Storico Domenicano).

Megaw, H. "The Chronology of Some Middle-Byzantine Churches." *Annual of the British School at Athens* 32 (1931–32):90–130.

Mélanges Soteriou: "Timetikos G. Soteriou" [In honor of G. Soteriou]. *Deltion Christianikes Archaiologikes Hetaireias*, 4th ser., 4 (1964–65). Athens, 1966.

Miller, William. *Essays on the Latin Orient*. Amsterdam, 1964.

———. "Ithaca and the Franks." *English Historical Review* 21 (1906):513–17.

———. "The Genoese in Chios, 1346–1556." *English Historical Review* 30 (1915):418–32.

———. *The Latins in the Levant: A History of Frankish Greece, 1204–1566*. London, 1908.

Millet, G. "L'école grecque dans l'architecture byzantine." In *Bibliothèque de l'Ecole des Hautes Etudes: Sciences Religieuses*, vol. 24. Paris, 1916.

———. *Le monastère de Daphni*. Paris, 1899.

Moutsopoulos, N. K. "Frangikes Ekklesies sten Hellada" [Frankish churches in Greece]. *Technika Chronika* 1 (1960):13–33.

———. "Le monastère franc de Notre Dame d'Isova, Gortynie." *Bulletin de Correspondance Héllenique* 80 (1956):76–94.

Muntaner, Ramon. *Chronik des edlen En Muntaner*. Bibliothek des literarischen Vereins, vol. 8, ed. K. Lanz. Stuttgart, 1844.

Neroutsos, T. D. "Christian Athens." *Bulletin of the Historical and Ethnological Society of Greece*, vol. 3 (1889); vol. 4 (1892).

Orlandos, A. "Anaskafai Stymphalou." In *Praktika tis Archaiologikis Hetaireias*, pp. 134–39. Athens, 1925.

———. "He Eccklesia tes Hagias Paraskeves: He Xylostegos Vasilike" [The church of Hagia Paraskeve: The wooden-roofed basilica]. *Hellenike Geografike Hetaireia*, 1922.

———. "He Frangike Ekklesia tes Stymfalias" [The Frankish church of Stymfalia]. In *Mélanges offerts à Octave et Melpo Merlier*, 1:118. Athens, 1955.

———. "He Hagia Theodora tes Artes" [The Hagia Theodora of Arta]. In *Archeion Vyzantinon Mnemeion tes Hellados*, pp. 88–104. Athens, 1936.

———. "Mesaionika Mnemeia Oropou kai Sykaminou" [Medieval monuments of Oropos and Sykaminos]. *Deltion Christianikes Archaiologikes Hetaireias*, ser. B, issue 4 (1927):25–45.

———. *Monuments byzantins de Chios*. Vols. 1 and 2 Athens, 1930.

———. "Neotera Evremata eis ten Monen Dafniou" [Recent findings at the monastery of Daphni]. *Archeion Vyzantinon Mnemeion tes Hellados* 8 (1955–56).

———. *He Omorfe Ekklesia*. Athens, 1921.

———. "Ta palatia kai Spitia tou Mystra" [Palaces and houses of Mystra]. *Archeion Vyzantinon Mnemeion tes Hellados*, 1937.

———. *He Paregoritissa tes Artes* [The Paregoritissa of Art]. Athens, 1963.

———. "Ai Vlachernai tes Eleias." *Archaeologiki Ephemeris*. Athens, 1923.

———. "Vyzantinoi Naoi tes Anatolikes Korinthias" [Byzantine churches of eastern Corinthia]. In *Archeion Vyzantinon Mnemeion tes Hellados* 1 (1935):118.

Papadakis, N. *He Ekklesia Kretes: Episkopai, Monai* [The church of Crete: Bishoprics, monasteries]. Canea, Crete, 1936.

Papageorgiou, Sp. *Historia tes Ekklesias tes Kerkyras* [History of the church of Corfu]. Athens, 1920.

Potthast, A. *Regesta pontificum Romanorum inde ab anno post Christum natum 1198 ad 1304.* Berlin, 1874–75.

Pouqueville, F. C. H. *Voyage de la Grèce.* 2d ed. 6 vols. Paris, 1820–26.

Pressuti, P. *Regestum Honorii III.* 2 vols. Rome, 1885–95.

Rodd, Sir Rennell. *The Princes of Achaea and the Chronicle of Morea.* London, 1907.

Romanini, A. M. *L'Architecture Gotica in Lombardia.* Rome, 1964.

Rose, H. *Die Baukunst der Cistercienser.* Munich, 1916.

Rottiers, B. E. A. *Description des monuments de Rhodes.* Brussels, 1828–30.

Santifaller, L. *Geschichte des lateinischen Patriarchats.* Weimer, 1938.

Schlumberger, G. *Expédition des Amulgavares où routiers catalans en Orient de l'an 1302 à l'an 1311.* Paris, 1902.

Schurenberg, L. *Die kirchliche Baukunst Frankreichs: 1270–1380.* Berlin, 1934.

Sejalon, H. "Institutions du chapitre général cistercien." In *Monasticon cisterciense,* ed. E. Solesmes. Rome: Typographeo Sancti Petri, 1892.

Sessevalle, F. de. *Histoire générale de l'ordre de Saint François.* Paris, 1935.

Setton, K. M. "The Latins in Greece and the Aegean from the Fourth Crusade to the End of the Middle Ages." Vol. 4, part 1 of the *Cambridge Medieval History.* Cambridge: At the University Press, 1966.

———. *Catalan Domination of Athens, 1311–1388.* Cambridge, Mass., 1948.

Smith, A. C. *The Architecture of Chios.* London, 1962.

Soteriou, G. A. *Christianike kai Vyzantine Archaiologia.* Athens, 1942.

Southern, R. W. *Western Society and the Church in the Middle Ages.* Harmondsworth, England: Penquin Books, 1970.

Spanaki, S. "Symbole sten Ekklesiastike Historia tes Kretes kata ten Venetokratia" [Contribution to the history of the church of Crete during the Venetian occupation]. In *Kretika Chronika* 3 (September–December 1959):243–88.

Spon, J., and Wheeler, G. *Voyage d'Italie, de Dalmatie, de Grèce, 1678–79.* Vol. 2. Amsterdam, 1679.

"Statuta generalia ordinis, edita in capitulis generalibus celebratis: Narbonnae an. 1260, Assissii an. 1279, atque Parisiis, an. 1292." *Archivo Franciscanum Historicum.* Collegium S. Bonaventura Quaracci, Italy, 1908.

Stikas, E. "Stereosis kai Apokatastasis tou Exonarthekos tou Katholikou tes Mones Daphniou" [Fastening and reconstruction of the outer narthex of the catholikon of the monastery of Daphni]. *Deltion tes Christianikes Archaiologikes Hetaireias,* 4th ser. Athens, 1962.

Strygowski, J. "Palaia Vyzantine Vasilike en Chalkidi" [The old Byzantine basilica of Chalkis]. In *Deltion tes Historikes kai Ethnologikes Hetaireias Hellados,* vol. 2. Athens, 1886.

Tafel, G. L., and Thomas, G. M. *Urkunden zur alteren Handels und Staatsgeschichte der Republik Venedig mit besonderer Beziehung auf Byzanz und die Levante.* 3 vols. Vienna, 1856–57.

Theocharis, Th. "He Xylostegos Vasilike tes Hagias Paraskeves Halkidos" [The wooden-roofed basilica of Hagia Paraskeve of Chalkis]. In *Archeion Euboikon Meleton,* pp. 140–56. Athens, 1960.

Thiriet, Fr. *La Romanie vénitienne au moyen âge: Le développement et l'exploitation du domaine colonial vénitien (12e–15e siècles).* Bibliothèque des Ecoles françaises d'Athènes et de Rome. Paris, 1959.

Thirion, J. *L'ancienne église de Lamourguier.* Le Roussillon, 1954.

Topping, P. "Co-existence of Greeks and Latins in Frankish Morea and Venetian Crete." In *15e Congrès International d'Etudes Byzantines: Rapports et co-rapports.* Athens, 1976.

Traquair, R. "Frankish Architecture in Greece." *Journal of the Royal Institute of British Architects,* 3d ser., vol. 31 (1923), nos. 2 and 3 (London).

————. "Medieval Fortresses of North Western Peloponnesus." *Annual of the British School of Archaeology* 13 (1906–7):268–81.

Tsirpanlis, N. "Nea Stoicheia Sketika me ten Ekklesiastiken Historian tes Venetokratoumenes Kretes 13os–17os Aionas apo Anecdota Venetika Engrafa" [New elements relative to the ecclesiastical history of Crete during the Venetian occupation, 13th and 14th centuries, from unpublished Venetian documents]. *Hellenika* 20 (1967):42–106.

Typaldos, G. E. "The Frankish Coat of Arms of Chalkis." *Annual of Byzantine Studies,* vol. 4 (1927).

Utley, F. L., ed. *Symposium: The Forward Movement of the Fourteenth Century.* Columbus: Ohio State University Press, 1961.

Valenciennes, Henri, de. "Une église de Notre Dame." In *Documents relatifs à l'histoire des Croisades,* ed. J. Longnon. Paris, 1948.

————. "L'histoire de l'empereur Henri de Constantinople." In *Documents relatifs á l'histoire des Croisades,* ed. J. Longnon. Paris, 1948.

Van der Vat, O. *Die Anfänge der Franziskanermissionen und ihre Weiterentwicklung in nahen Orient und in der Mohammedanischen Ländern während des 13 Jahrhunderts.* Werl, Westfallen: Franziskus–Drückerei, 1934.

Villehardouin, Geoffrey. *De la conquête de Constantinople par les barons français associés aux Vénitiens l'an 1204.* Edited by E. Faral. 2 vols. Paris, 1938–39.

Viollet-le-Duc, E. *Dictionnaire raisonné de l'architecture française du 11e au 16e siècle.* 10 vols. Paris, 1854.

Wace, A. J. B. "Frankish Sculpture at Parori, Geraki." *Annual of the British School of Athens* 11 (1904–5):139–45.

Wadding, L. *Annales minorum seu trium ordinum.* Rome, 1731–1886.

Walz, P. A. M. *Compendium historiae ordinis praedicatorum,* pp. 163–65. Rome, 1948.

Weltet, Th. "Un recueil d'exemple du 13e siècle." *Etudes Françiscanes* 30 (1913):648–49.

White, J. *Italian Art and Architecture, 1250–1400.* London, 1966.

Wolff, R. L. "The Latin Empire of Constantinople and the Franciscans." *Traditio* 2 (1944):221 (New York: Fordham University Press).

————. "Romania: The Latin Empire of Constantinople." *Speculum* 23 (1948):1–34.

Xanthoudides, Stephanos. "He Venetokratia en Krete kai oi kata ton Eneton Agones ton Kreton" [The Venetian occupation of Crete and the struggle of the Cretans against the Venetians]. *Byzantinische Neugriechische Jahrbücher,* no. 39 (Athens, 1939).

Xygopoulos, A. "To Templon tes Hagias Paraskeves en Chalkidi" [The templum of Hagia Paraskeve in Chaliks]. *Deltion Christianikes Archaiologikes Hetaireias* 4 (1927):67.

———. "Vyzantinoi Naoi Metaskevasmenoi" [Reconstructed Byzantine churches]. In *Deltion Christianikes Archaiologikes Hetaireias* (1931), p. 67.

Y Luch, Antonio Rubio. *Katalonika Frouria eis ten Hepeirotiken Hellada* [Catalonian castles in continental Greece]. Translated by G. Mavrakis. In *Hestia*. Athens, 1912.

———. "Los Navarros en Grecia y el Ducado Catalan de Atenas en la epoca de su invasion." In *Memorios de la Real Academia de Buenas Letras*. Barcelona, 1886.

Zakythinos, D. *Le despotat grec de Morée*. Paris, 1932.

Index

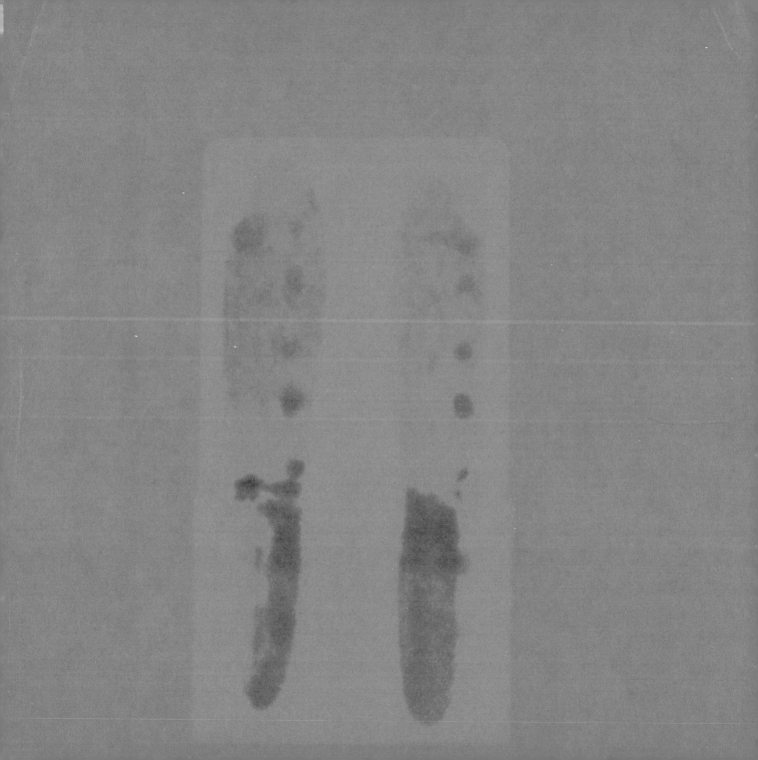